Hope Inside Out
Approaching Depression with Purposeful Hope

JULIE THOMAS

WESTBOW
PRESS*
A DIVISION OF THOMAS NELSON
& ZONDERVAN

WestBow Press books may be ordered through booksellers or by contacting:

WestBow Press
A Division of Thomas Nelson & Zondervan
1663 Liberty Drive
Bloomington, IN 47403
www.westbowpress.com
1 (866) 928-1240

Because of the dynamic nature of the Internet, any web addresses or links contained in this book may have changed since publication and may no longer be valid. The views expressed in this work are solely those of the author and do not necessarily reflect the views of the publisher, and the publisher hereby disclaims any responsibility for them.

Cover design by Julie Thomas.

Author photo by Niji Stanley.

Scripture quotations are taken from the Holy Bible, New Living Translation, copyright ©1996, 2004, 2007, 2013, 2015 by Tyndale House Foundation. Used by permission of Tyndale House Publishers, Inc., Carol Stream, Illinois 60188. All rights reserved.

Scripture quotations taken from the Amplified® Bible (AMP), Copyright © 2015 by The Lockman Foundation. Used by permission. www.Lockman.org.

Scripture quotations from THE MESSAGE. Copyright © by Eugene H. Peterson 1993, 1994, 1995, 1996, 2000, 2001, 2002. Used by permission of NavPress. All rights reserved. Represented by Tyndale House Publishers, Inc.

Taken from the Complete Jewish Bible by David H. Stern. Copyright © 1998. All rights reserved. Used by permission of Messianic Jewish Publishers, 6120 Day Long Lane, Clarksville, MD 21029. www.messianicjewish.net.

Scripture quotations marked (ESV) are from the ESV® Bible (The Holy Bible, English Standard Version®), copyright © 2001 by Crossway, a publishing ministry of Good News Publishers. Used by permission. All rights reserved.

ISBN: 978-1-5127-8183-0 (sc)
ISBN: 978-1-5127-8184-7 (hc)
ISBN: 978-1-5127-8182-3 (e)

Library of Congress Control Number: 2017904695

Print information available on the last page.

WestBow Press rev. date: 5/25/2017

Dedication

A dedication is incomplete without wholeheartedness. To my Father in heaven who never let go of my hands, this is wholeheartedly yours.

A dedication is incomplete without commitment and sacrifice. And three precious people in my life that paid that price, forbearing the fiercest storms of my journey by my side, I dedicate this to you – my Chach (Mathew), my Jude, my Seth.

And once again a dedication is incomplete without determination and perseverance, to all the persevering women I've met and those I have not, those still continuing to push through the dark days of depression, this is for you.

Gratitude

Call me incomplete if I did not have these people in my life to write each chapter of some of my darkest years. You are the ones I acknowledge because, without you all I would not have survived this depression, nor would this book have been realized. From the bottom of my heart I thank God for you.

To my spiritual mother, my mentor, my life coach and my biggest cheer leader – Dr Neecie. Thank you for walking with me, understanding every inch of my pain and lovingly guiding me through it all.

To my pastor - Pastor Kendall. Right from the day you knew of my struggle to the present, thank you for your prayers over me, over my home, for encouraging my spiritual desires even through my limitations.

To each one of my lovely sister friends – my life group girls, for accepting me despite knowing my weaknesses, for the tremendous time, words of courage and love each one of you have given me, I am grateful.

To my wonderful friends, prayer partners and leaders at Freedom Church, that have known my story, that have spoken hope and destiny into this broken story – you know who you are, thank you all.

To my fellow life coaches and friends at Life Coaching, you provided a secure platform for me to unveil my vulnerabilities and life challenges, shouldered me through it all, until I reached the other side. Thank you coaches.

To my dear parents, my two loving sisters, my two brothers-in-love, and my sweet nieces and nephew- thank you so much for loving, supporting and cheering me on towards my dreams.

To my cousins – who spoke into my life, and told me time after time to go after it, and to step into my calling, also for the warm meals, thank you cousins.

To some of my closest friends- who saw this struggle rising even before I did, helped me, prayed over me unrelentingly, cried with me, walked with me every step of the way, and continuing to walk –thank you dear friends.

To my husband – for sticking with me through the storm, for pushing me to go after my dreams, for dedicating many hours to our home and children, so that I could pursue my dreams. To my Jude for caring for mama when she was physically weak, for encouraging me to go after my dreams, for applauding every little thing mama did. To my Seth, for telling me "don't give up mama" even when you saw my strength fail, and for laying your hands on mama and praying for me – I cannot thank God enough for all three of you.

Endorsement

Dr. Julie Thomas is not only a prolific writer, but she has an anointing to speak words of truth. In this book, there is practical, godly wisdom that will lead you down a path where you will find freedom from fear, as your hope is renewed and restored. My prayer is that you will not keep this book to yourself. I hope you will look for thousands who are dying spiritually and emotionally, desperately needing to hear the words contained in this brilliantly anointed book.

Dr. Neecie Moore
Life Coaching Institute
www.lifecoaching.institute

Foreword

We all face trials of different kinds. We all experience tragedy, hurts, abuse, unfairness, pain, difficulties and struggles of various measure. In each war that we wage, we desperately try to find help from someone who has gone through what we are facing. Far too often, no one is willing to speak about the things that show our weaknesses and vulnerability. We are afraid to be perceived as frail, unable to cope and desperate. In "Hope Inside Out," Dr. Julie Thomas takes off the mask. She shares the innermost battle of her soul. She allows you to see inside her raw and real warfare with a most persistent enemy. The truths that are captured in these pages that follow, will give you the hope that you need to rise above your storm. There will be moments when you say, "Finally someone understands." You will think, "At last, someone has tapped into the world that I am living." But most importantly, you will find the tools to allow you to conquer and overcome your own nightmare. Get ready for a journey through the battlefield of the mind. Only this time, you have a friend walking with you. Get ready to experience Hope, Inside Out.

Kendall Bridges
Lead Pastor
Freedom Church
www.findfreedom.church

Contents

CHAPTER 1
Journal Letters

If God has shown us bad times ahead, it's
enough for me that He knows about them
—Corrie Ten Boom

Quivering, gasping for breath, I felt the tingle from the cold night air against the sweat on my brow and the chill of the stone pavement beneath my bare feet. The stirring from the raging thoughts in my mind were coming to a calm. I had to stop running now as my mind steered back to the reality of where I stood.

The reflection from the street lamp at the base of which I halted was sufficient for me to gather a visible range of my surroundings—enough to realize that I was alone and that it was sometime during the night hours. Soon enough, a passing cold draft also brought me about to realize that I did all that running without the needed layering to brace the cold.

I had stopped long enough to recover my breath

A whole week of struggling, mentally, physically, and emotionally, has passed. Struggle continues. I don't want to struggle anymore.

and turned around to retrace my steps. Retracing footsteps seemed simpler than retracing the mind's steps. Retracing footsteps meant I would just have to run those steps back, albeit barefoot. The mind's steps—those would hurt more than the cold, coarse sidewalk, grazing against the soles of my feet. Muffled memory pulled me home, where I remembered leaving two babies and a husband, following a mental and emotional breakdown on my part. I have yet to recall what triggered the outburst. All I am able to recall is the harrowing fear and tempest of the mind that led the way for my sprinting out the door and into the night.

I ran as fast as I could and as hard as I could. What was I running from? I did not know. My mind was not able to cooperate with the backdrop of my home and my family. Everything at home had begun to increasingly overwhelm my mind. I know today that the running was a means of escape from whatever was causing anguish to my mind. Only, when my family found me and took me home, the anguish trailed home with me.

Running failed to exhaust the anguish. The only one exhausted was me. How I wished that I had never stopped running. All my yearning was for all this to pass. It was intensely painful to live inside of myself— with the depression.

Sad . . . really sad for the past few days. No one to understand. And I cannot explain this either. Still believing for healing.

As I gaze into the beautiful brown eyes of my children today, I hope to God that nothing that transpired in the past five years has settled anywhere in their hearts. The birth of my second son is what propelled the beginning of an aching chapter in my life. It was the beginning of depression. It was an illness of the mind, which I was completely ignorant about. And I never expected to become victim to the unfortunate impressions it left on a person.

I came home from spending three days in the hospital with my new bundle of joy. Little did I know I was also bringing home another bundle—of sadness. A heartache that I felt utterly guilty about expressing to anyone. What mother would pair sadness with the joy of cuddling a newborn child? In all honesty, I did embrace the joys of childbirth. But it was always accompanied by sadness—sadness I could not comprehend.

With each passing day after my son's birth, I began to feel blurry and delusional. One of my delusions included the hospital hallway. I would see the hallway time and again. I did "leave" the hospital. My mind, however, tarried on the postpartum-floor hallway. I could see myself pacing up and down

Woke up feeling empty and sad. I'm pouring out everything before You, Lord.

Lord, consider my heart today. Please take away the heaviness that has lingered for so long. Even as my heart and mind draws closer to You, the heaviness presses more.

the corridor, like I was in search of something. What I was searching for … I did not know. I truly did not. I sensed a gloom, a reverie, that I had left something behind. The pacing I was envisioning kept playing in my mind, like a broken record. It was like hitting rewind and then play on a movie clip, repeatedly. All of this was delusion. Delusion that had in all its falsity become a disturbing reality to my mind.

I am able to reflect back on and chronicle this today. But the season when the delusions were active was a time during which I was unable to entirely keep track of myself, my surroundings, my family, and my life.

While I was already weathering the blow from all of those events, my perturbed mind had started to believe that I had wronged my child—a child who was absolutely whole. I felt morally responsible for the premature birth of my son. I would mourn over my baby as though I had lost him. I was convinced that his premature birth was due to lack of care and nurturing from his mama. It was

I can do nothing on my own. My frailty is evident with each passing day, just as my dependency increases each day.

at this point we discerned that we needed some medical assistance. Up until then, we were battling with denial.

I was diagnosed with postpartum depression. Consequently, I was started on prescription medications to treat the symptoms. However, the symptoms that would not succumb to treatment began to multiply. Alongside postpartum depression came another diagnosis, of fibromyalgia. This disorder causes widespread pain all over the body, along with chronic fatigue, sleeplessness, and the like. The level of intensity of this kind of pain made me sensitive even to the slightest touch and oftentimes left me incapable of normal movement.

Add to this my two babies and graduate school, and it was as though overnight, I was camped under a canopy of stress. Until now, I had not known what it was like to have poor health. My reality was shifting—and not for the better. I dragged myself through the routines within the house—kids, cooking, school, laundry, etc. But my routines and reality all seemed like they were ringing from a distance, far away from my mind. I had to forcefully bring my mind to the chore at hand to be able to function. I don't know if this even makes sense. Somehow, the delusions had become my reality, and my reality had become my delusions.

I was oftentimes nauseated and vomited a lot. It wasn't a digestive disorder as we suspected. The level of fear and anxiety was just that overwhelming. I despised it. I didn't have a clue as to what to do about it. Everything around me, including the walls in my home, seemed like they were

Woke up today, without sleep most of the night, physically miserable. Mentally exhausted.

caving in on me. I felt claustrophobic in my own home. I felt trapped.

Nesting in this anguish was dreadful. I was afraid of myself—afraid of hurting my family. The innocent faces of my little ones startled me so many times. And then, there were the surreal moments when my mind would draw a blank, to the point of sometimes not being able to recognize my own children. Tell that to any devoted mother, and she would tell you that would be immensely disturbing and heartbreaking.

Little did I know that the birth of a baby would wreak so much havoc on my mind and body. The toll on the physical body was a combination of nausea, vomiting, dizziness, sleeplessness, loss of appetite, and the resulting weakness. Often these symptoms sprang up all together. Several hours of the night would be spent wakeful. A lot of the times I spent the entire night with eyes wide open and resisting the bidding of sweet sleep. If and when I did receive the rare gift of sleep, it was almost always disconnected by frightful nightmares.

All the symptoms and reactions of my body were of secondary concern to me—secondary to an emotional stirring. A stirring, a derangement of the mind that left me lamenting my very being.

I am losing all hope; I am paralyzed with fear . . . Come quickly, LORD, and answer me, for my depression deepens. Don't turn away from me, or I will die. (Psalm 143:4, 7 NLT)

Notice that this particular woe of depression was borrowed from David and the book of Psalms. I

Feeling so far and empty and so far from You, I feel like You are far away, Lord! I'm waiting with pain in my heart.

always attributed the verses in scripture to strength, faith, and hope. Growing up, I memorized memory verses, participated in scripture memory competitions, and the like. As a child, I don't recall having memorized a verse that sounded even remotely close to the one we read here. I would read the word on a regular basis. In fact, I read it every day if I could make it happen. My regular reading, however, was aimed toward the parables, the miracle stories, the powerful leaders, of which the word has plenty to portray. No harm there. It is always uplifting to read stories of valor and supernatural miracles. The harm here, however, was in how I was looking at the word. I was looking at it through a lens of perfection, of power and the paranormal. I did not believe there was room for weakness, hopelessness, and depression anywhere in the context of the word.

When we consider the word, even among the accounts of miracles, there typically is mention of a problem. The problematic scene usually marks the arrival of Jesus or a prophet like Elijah or Elisha, among many others. More often than not, straightaway there is a miracle recorded for the pages of history. What is not recorded in many instances is the agonizing state of heart of the individuals engaged in these scenarios. What was their pain like? Were they wearied in appearance? What were their lives like during

A place of confusion and lostness today. Holy Spirit, uphold me, never to fall back, only to push forward.

the life of their problem? You know—the raw pains and struggles.

Take the life of Moses as an illustration. We read about his life in the pharaoh's palace, and the next thing we know is that after an incident of conflict, he is in the wilderness among a group of people, where he finds a wife and starts a career tending to sheep. What we do not read in connection to his history is how he spent the forty years after he left the palace. He only returned to the pharaoh forty years after his escape from palatial life. Besides sheep tending and being a family man, what did his life resemble? I often wonder if he ever wished to go back to the life in the palace—if he ever yearned to read the finest of scholarly material he was once privileged to access, that belonged to the richest civilization in the world at the time, all while herding his smelly flock. Was he ever brokenhearted and sad? In all reality, he probably did experience one or more of those emotions. We can only ponder over what came to pass during the interval of the second half of Moses' story.

My perception of the word and the tone I received from it, was one of exceptional will and strength. I saw no room for frailty. It wasn't until depression became an integral part of my life that I began to dive deeper into the pages. Depression had by now become a way of life to me. A good number of my days were spent in the

Struggle still on. I have to push through. But I can't fight anymore, God. You have to fight for me.

throes and woes of the illness. So naturally, as I turned to the pages of scripture, even as I yearned for the powerful verses that brought relief and hope, I embarked on a search for verses of pain, sorrow, and real struggle. What I found was several proses of melancholy like the verses penned by David.

The journal entries you see in this chapter (except for the one cited earlier from the Psalms) are selected excerpts from my personal journal. Words of dejection and melancholy that I found strikingly similar to the ones in scripture. I began to observe a pattern, a connection between the writings in my journal and the scriptures. The pages and verses began to come alive before my eyes. How had I not seen that before?

The only explanation I could gather for that question was that I had never been to a place of such desperation before this. It was a degree of desperation that would send me in search of hope, comfort, and more importantly, compatibility in real, raw struggles. It brought me such solace as I followed along the purely transparent words of the heroes of the Bible. Transparency that enabled me to see who they truly were, even with the valiance attached to their names. The majority of us who name our kids after these heroes name them in attribution with their heroic traits rather than their nonheroic ones, don't we? Who would want to associate themselves with weakness?

Heartbroken, Lord!
Struggling to get up from
this one. This I know, that I
will not give up my hope in
You. But I need You now. I
need You to walk with me.
Heal the pain of my heart.
Comfort the wounds,
and show me Your way.

I think God did. He wanted to associate with our weakness. Why else would He, among the magnanimity of His promises and wonders, insert morsels of stories of human fragility? He had royalty author the most intimate pains and secrets of his heart through the pen of King David. He sent us the Servant King, who trekked the earth and lived a life, with no home to call His own or a place to lay His head at night.

> "And Jesus told him 'Foxes have holes and the birds of the air have nests, but the Son of Man has nowhere to lay his head'" (Luke 9:58 AMP).

I cannot convey well enough how much these words of weakness and depression meant to me in the middle of my suffocating struggle. Their humanity and weakness speaks volumes more than the victories that made them people of reputation. It validates that these were people just like you and me and had to make it through their season of testing to arrive at their season of greatness. I have the privilege of expounding on the stories of some of these heroes in later chapters.

In the meanwhile, I will draw further into my season

of weakness because we can only appreciate hope when we have seasons of hopelessness to weigh against them. We ought to know what it is like to be weak in order to respect strength—to know that darkness always precedes the light. That our seasons of hopelessness, weakness, and darkness are also worth gathering, for without them we can never fully appreciate the comforting relief we experience when we are free.

To say the least, the residual effect of my depression struggle was swiftly transferring itself into the walls of my home. Our home has plenty of windows to let in light—but I would not have them open. The drapes were always closed. The light troubled me. The outside troubled me. It may be irony speaking when I say I was content in my misery, mostly because of fear and doubt, of what uncertainty the outside would hold. I tucked myself within the walls of my home—a home where I wasn't feeling all that settled or secure either. But that seemed less intimidating than the outside. Darkness had encompassed me, mentally and literally.

If God had showed me these dark times ahead, I'm not certain I would have been willingly recruited for all that passed in my life. Then again, I must step back and reflect—shouldn't it be enough for me that He knows about it? That He will be there with me?

When we live in a home with

Broken and tired, Lord,
You put the broken
pieces together, back
as You see fit.

family around us, we are not the only ones entrenched in the residual misery. It could affect not just your family but your friends and colleagues, among others. When my mind was in turmoil, my family was also consequently trapped in at least some parts of the turmoil, if not all, as is evident from my running episode introduced in the beginning of the chapter.

My husband once told me at about the midpoint of my struggle that he would secretly pray and ask God for a sign of my forthcoming healing. He asked that I would one day draw those drapes aside myself—that I would welcome the light into our home myself. This drawing of the drapes, he said, would be to him a sign that my healing was unfolding.

CHAPTER 2
Hiding Place

But when anything is exposed and reproved by
the light, it is made visible and clear, and where
everything is visible and clear, there is light.
—Ephesians 5:13 AMPC

By light of day, everything seemed fine. I put on smiles, albeit strained. I tried to look my best and smile my best, so no one would catch the weighed-down state of my heart in my eyes. My façade resulted in the caving in of any physical and emotional strength I may have had in my possession. And it wasn't like I had much to spare. I felt like I needed to convince others that I wasn't weak. Every part of being *normal* in life became not normal—undoable. As much as I tried to appear as perfect as possible on the outside, nothing inside me was even remotely close to that.

I did not want to see or interact with people. Routine visits to the grocery store were very unnerving. Again, the lights troubled me. The lights, the sounds, the people, the aisles … everything seemed like it was spinning before my eyes. The sounds of grocery carts banging and chatter going back and forth would all keep echoing and reechoing in my ears. All the sounds and lights combined would drown out my mind. It was all I could do to gather my supersensitized self and scramble out of there. Even something as elementary and routine to everyday life as the sound of my cell phone ringing would startle me to verge of panic. So much so that I kept my cell phone ringer off for most of the years of my struggle.

> Surely the darkness will cover me, and
> the night will be the only light around me.
> (Psalm 139:11 AMP)

What the psalmist said here was precisely, verbatim, how I felt. I was withdrawing, and embedding into darkness, isolating myself. Inside of me there was yearning that this would pass—that the darkness would go away. But the dark prevailed for over five long years. I would look around at my surroundings, my circumstances, and myself and wonder, "What perceivable good or purpose could come from a place like this?" There couldn't possibly be a good reason for all this suffering.

It was a deep pit experience. The pit was dark and lonely and had evolved into a premise for emotional and mental torment. A pit experience that brought me face to face with my Maker. I was so angry with Him for what I was going through. Did He not see the fears, the suffering, the many sleepless nights? The struggle was ongoing, year after year. *Darkness* and *Fear* had become the antagonists in my story.

The extended years of being in this pit of depression also brought me face to face with myself. I did not want to live with me. Anymore. The only way out of this dark pit was if life ended. That was the only path that was visible to me. The only path that *Dark* let me see was one of mortality. The *Dark* in front of me won, and I followed in a trance several times. With hope that I would drown in a sleep that would not hurt anymore. But medications that caused me to faint with consumption of just the regular dosage did nothing to me when the entire dose was exhausted. It did nothing. Now I was afraid of myself.

Fear had become my worst rival and started to manifest its power on my body. My chest felt like it had a ton of bricks weighing it down. It made it hard to breathe some days. *Fear* told me I was worthless. For the entire duration of my struggle, I lived in relentless fear.

Fear and *Dark* were now working hand in hand in my life. I felt helpless and defenseless both on the inside and out.

I was longing for a way to step into the light. How could I do that when everything around me was being serenaded by the night of depression? If there exists something called hitting your lowest point, then I had. I had never imagined for myself, even in my wildest dreams, a life filled with so much despair—unexplainable despair.

Despair is relevant in situations of harsh poverty, the death of a loved one, a terminal illness, or devastation of home and property through calamity. None of these grave scenarios were applicable to me. I mean, it would make sufficient sense if my despair was equalized by one or any of those misfortunes. My low point could not be explained, and my state of mind could not be construed in the intellectual sense.

Corrie Ten Boom knew and experienced pain and despair firsthand. She lays it all out in black and white in her book *The Hiding Place*. This watchmaker's family risked their lives during World War II to save the lives of as many Jews as they could. Hitting one low point after the other, as she and her family endured the misery of a war-soaked time. Corrie survived the concentration camps, thinking at each point of lowness that it couldn't get any worse. She had been battered to a wretched state.

Her story in *The Hiding Place* is filled with gold nuggets of her experiences and lessons of how she took every low point and envisioned some good budding out of it for herself and for the glory of God. The Ten Boom family was well aware of the risk of being discovered because of their risky venture. They had to collectively, as a family, come to a point of contemplation on whether they should continue to give refuge to people in their home. Corrie, her father, and her sister, Betsie, came together in prayer and decided that they had to move forward with the chancy mission. Corrie remarked, "Perhaps only when human effort had *done its best and failed*, would God's power alone be free to work."

Their home was raided the next day after the family made this decision, and they were taken as prisoners. Her purpose, however, did not end at the brunt of the arrest. She continued to find purpose in every debasing, revolting condition she was thrown into throughout her captivity.

I believe in the power of prayer, but it appeared that it was resisting its functionality in my life. And believe me, I got a lot of prayer from some amazing spiritual leaders. These were amazing pastors who took on a sincere commitment to see me healed. Everyone who prayed for me told me that there would be a purpose to my pain. I heard this enough times to plant in me the seed of purpose. From all this pain, both physical and emotional, a purpose?

In my case, every possible human effort was made, and it had "done its best and failed"—doctors' visits, medications, tests, scans, my prayers, others prayers, all futile. I even picked up learning guitar in an attempt to keep my mind distracted from the senseless, irrational, disruptive thoughts. I took up art and tried my hand at making creative, abstract pieces of canvas art. Anything to preserve the remnants of whatever sanity I had remaining. Well, art and guitar didn't turn out as I had hoped.

I was trying to find or make my purpose happen on my own. I was genuinely invested in knowing what that purpose was, which people reiterated. But all the trying to make my purpose happen only wearied me more. I know—you must be thinking, *A guitar? And art? How tiring could that be?* However that may be, I had pushed an already impoverished mind to plummet even further. Every effort I made to overcome my malady had "done its best and failed."

The struggle appeared unbeatable and was becoming more unbearable with each passing day. Emotionally I was distraught, physically overwrought. Why could I not step out of this depression and darkness? How could I continue to live this way?

> The heart truly is hopelessly dark and deceitful, a puzzle that no one can figure out. (Jeremiah 17:9 The Message)

The villainous *Fear* … it thrives in the dark. It engulfs us in the solace of the dark. And we become so afraid and uncertain of the changes that may ensue if we step out of the shadow and gloom, that we nest there. *It's safer here in the dark*, we tend to think. *I'm familiar with my misery. What if stepping out into the light causes things to sway toward more pain?* These were all interrogations I had for myself. We stay hidden for so long, and before we know it, the safety of our existing, familiar, dark place becomes our *hiding* place.

Unbeknownst to us, these lies become our hiding place. When we tell ourselves that it's all right to isolate ourselves from everyone and everything around us. Depression begins to narrow us into our hiding place. We're cornered into a hiding place that has evolved into our misery, yet has become our familiarity. There resides the lie. Our hiding place translates into a place of false refuge.

In the scripture I shared above, I related my experience to what the psalmist talked about, "darkness" covering him, and "the night will be the only dark around me." He doesn't stop there, though. He goes on to deliberate more about the creator of darkness and light.

> Even the darkness is not dark to You and conceals nothing from You. But the night shines as bright as the day; Darkness and light are alike to You. (Psalm 139:12 AMP)

Everything we see in creation are details that He called out of the darkness into the light. It was all dark. The scriptures say in Genesis that there was a void. Darkness covered the earth until God said, "Let there be light!" He sees everything, even when we think we are submerged in darkness.

What is awesome to see in this deliberation about light and dark is the distinction God Himself drew between the two. He separated the light and distinguished it from the darkness! It may be completely mundane to you and me, this distinction between the two. We see it happen every day. When the sun comes up, it's daytime, and when the sun goes down, it's nighttime. Even a toddler knows that. Nothing special, right?

But have you ever wondered why He did that? What is the purpose of the contrast between light and darkness? I think it was for our simple, human minds to comprehend the good, the revelation, that comes when we emerge from the dark. At sunrise, everything is illuminated under the light of the sun. At nightfall, everything is submerged in darkness from the lack of sunlight. A lamp brought into a room that is pitch dark gives the eyes a vision and perception of everything in the room.

You may be wondering, what good can come from this conversation about light and dark? When we nest in the dark, in the grimness of our hard situations, the inclination to dwell there is higher. The chance of prolonging the agony is higher. When we battle depression, the more we hide in the dark, the more our symptoms fester there. And with each passing day, it gets increasingly difficult to detach ourselves from them.

Now there is nothing wrong in having a hiding place. We all have our little hiding places—a place of solace or comfort. I love to cuddle up in a nook at my home with a blanket, a piece of chocolate, and a book. It's my comfort nook.

When it comes to depression, however, these hiding places may provide comfort, but they will also provide premise for isolation and withdrawal. We need to realize that the longevity of all hiding places is fleeting. The safety we feel in our hiding place of isolation is short-lived. There's only so much you can endure in hiding, when you're battling something that is capable of subduing you.

When I started my battle with postpartum depression, the first instinct that kicked in was "nobody should know about this." Both my husband and I gripped on to the same attitude—that no one needed to know about our battle with the demon that the depression had eventually become. Every challenge with the emotions, with the daily running of our household, the care of our kids … everything was swept under the rug. Great hiding place. And oh, the more we concealed it, the bigger the depression demon grew under the rug. Eventually everything we buried in the dark towered into a Goliath right before our eyes. Nothing we tried fit anymore. We felt like we were fighting more with ourselves rather than the enemy that stood before us. We were wearing the wrong armor—Saul's armor.

If you are familiar with the story of David and Goliath, then you know that Goliath was a giant from the enemy army who provoked the army of Israel to a one-on-one battle. The giant wanted a giant-to-man skirmish. And while Goliath was out there making a mockery of their army, every trained soldier on this side of camp faced a bigger giant. Intimidation. Fear.

There, out of this army of military men, emerged a shepherd boy who was only present at the battle site on account of delivering bread and cheese to his uniformed brothers. No one, including his own kin, would have given him a second look during this tense situation, let alone the unreal possibility of considering this thimble of a boy to combat this giant.

I wonder if David ever thought, at some point during this whole ordeal, that he might be insane or demented for thinking he could take this giant. I'm assuming that he probably did. I assume that only because he is human. The probability of that thought having grazed his mind is pretty high. Fear would have at the least teased him, if not terrified him. No person on earth is void of the feeling of fear.

But David, at some point during his shepherding, had to have come to the understanding that if he left himself to worry about his fear rather than the carnivore sniffing around his sheep, he wouldn't have many sheep left to take back to his father's sheepfold.

He had to face up to his fear, to be able to face up to the lamb-chop-craving canine.

Coming back from the fields to the battlefield, David was now decided and ready to combat the giant. King Saul heard of this young boy obviously and thought it best to send him out donned in the army's finest armor, the king's armor. As the not-so-tall boy slowly put on each piece of armor that belonged to the over six-foot-tall king, he would have visualized the clumsiness that would become of his trotting around in this oversized metallic suit. And still, in order to humor the king, he trotted anyway.

Both of them had to know this wouldn't work. Saul's armor did not fit this shepherd boy. And we all know the conclusion of this story. David confronted Goliath. Goliath was heavily brass clad on every part of his body, except a portion of his face. That opening was all David needed. David knew two things. One, he knew he didn't need an exaggerated military vest; he only needed his smooth stones and a sling. To aim for and strike the giant in the only spot that his armor didn't protect: right between the eyes. And second, he knew he had to first face up to his fear in order to face up to the giant.

Returning from the pages of biblical history to my story, I had to face up to my fear of confronting my giant: depression. I had to step out from the shadows and call this giant out for who it was. I had to address it for the evil mania it was, that was threatening to take down my mind and my sanity. And like David, I had to hit it in the spot that would be its undoing. I had to hit it in the shame, the fear, and the stigma. And I couldn't do it camouflaged under the wrong armor. My armor was me hiding behind all the pain and the shame. The more I concealed it, the heavier and harder it was to carry. Instead of battling my giant with a sling and a stone, I was doing some of the trotting around David was doing in Saul's armor. Only it was very painful trotting—physically and emotionally painful.

What armor are you hiding behind? Pain? Shame? Denial? Or … Humor? Pretend smiles? All this emphasis on light and dark, David and Goliath, and the armor and sling and stone is to reiterate, to reverberate the same truth. You need to step out of the shame and the stigma. You need to face up to your giant. Knock it down to the ground and trot your victory trot.

For over five years, I lived in fear and dread. I went to bed dreading the dawn of the morning hours. I woke up in dread. Many, many days passed where dread was my escort. Every day I woke up with a knot in my stomach. I lived every minute in the anticipation that something dreadful was about to unfold. I lived in constant dread, watching for the arrival of the next dreadful event.

These accounts that I share, none of them were conjured up. This was how I was living out my days. I tried almost unrelentingly to convince myself of the contrary. "I don't have to be afraid. I don't have to feel this way." Without question, I did not want to feel this way. If you could imagine how miserable it would be to live life this way, especially when you are not able to present evidence or reasonable grounds for feeling this way. But the feeling was every bit as real as breathing is to you and me.

One of the supporting pedestals for the fear in my life was the fear of people—and rightfully so, on many occasions. There have been individuals who weren't shy in dishing out their opinions and decrees on how I should and should not feel. Today I would ascribe their comments to either ignorance or plain insensitivity. But at the time, my mind didn't have the gathering to decipher it in this manner. To me, they were vexing an already injured soul.

If you are facing any sort of human judgment for your mental illness, and avoiding the person or persons is a feasibility, then do so at the least for that season. It is not worth sacrificing your mental and emotional sanity to please someone who may never understand or seek to understand your dejection.

> The fear of human opinion disables;
> trusting in God protects you from that.
> (Proverbs 29:25 The Message)

What if David had proceeded to hide behind what people thought of him—his brothers, his father, the king, not to leave out everyone else. Because let's face it, as per description, this boy was handsome, ruddy, and yet small. His stature, in every sense, did not match up to even what the prophet Samuel was expecting when he visited their home to anoint the next king of Israel. David's father had lined up the rest and best of his sons, beginning with the oldest and tallest, to be anointed king. David did not make the draft. And it was because they thought he was inadequate to face the giant, that he was asked to don the substantially taller king's armor.

David could not afford to hide behind the oversized armor, or he would never have been able to conclude the feat before him. And we, would have been deprived of the daring tale of David and Goliath. And Sunday school kids would have been deprived of the coloring pages that illustrate the story of the giant and the young boy who conquered the giant.

CHAPTER 3
Mirror, Mirror, on the Wall

Each hour I look aside
Upon my secret mirror
Trying all postures there
To make my image fair
—C. S. Lewis

The mirror from the classic fairy tale of all time, *Snow White and the Seven Dwarfs*, is familiar to most of us. The queen stepmother in the fairytale asked her magic mirror every day, "Mirror, mirror, on the wall. Who is the fairest one of all?" The mirror replied to her satisfaction every day. Until one day, the mirror gave her an answer that displeased her to the point of wrath. "Famed is thy beauty, majesty. But hold, a lovely maid I see. Rags cannot hide her gentle grace. Alas, she is more fair than thee." My identification with this fairytale has nothing to do with the seven dwarfs,

Prince Charming, or even the "happily ever after." The mirror. The mirror is the protagonist in my story.

Every day, you and I wake up to face a mirror, be it right above the sink, or the bedroom dresser. More often than not, first thing in the morning, a good majority of us look up to see our pillow-tousled hair and droopy faces in the mirror. That has become such an indispensable part of our human lives. One would consider it normal, wouldn't one? The mirror has become to some extent, an extension of our lives.

Now what if, one day, like Snow White's stepmother, we are unhappy with what our mirror says. We stare at the mirror. And the person staring back at us isn't happy with what he or she sees. Have you noticed that the reflection in our mirror poses the inverse of our image? The opposite - much like how a lot of us view ourselves. And we are unhappy with our mirror's response, much like the queen stepmother.

Over the past five years of my struggle with depression, I battled a lot with my reflection. I had reached a mark of such low self-worth that I started to shy away from myself. I started to shy away from the *me* in the mirror. I did not think the person staring back at me was worthy of eye contact. A fog of fear had clouded my eyes. The *me* staring back seemed blurry and hazy. I had actually figured out how to locate something wrong with everything about me— appearance, qualification, confidence, and on and on. I wasn't satisfied with the answer the *mirror on the wall* rendered back to me. When my inside was in disarray, it was bound to reflect on the outside.

Before long, I started to shy away from sitting in proximity to anyone because I didn't want them to see everything my mirror was showing me that I didn't like. I didn't want people to see the eclipse over my eyes or the inadequacies in me. And get this, it was as though that stack of insecurity wasn't sufficient. I ventured out to buy myself one of those countertop magnifying mirrors with inbuilt lighting. This was the first time that I used a mirror of this kind. Obviously I was pea-brained and mindless at the time of this purchase. Why would I do that at a time when I was already having a persuasion-dissuasion war with myself about my self-worth? A mirror that magnifies every tiny pore on my face! I can laugh about it now, but that one haunted me for weeks!

My mirror also brought me face-to-face, head-to-head with me. I did *not* want to live with me—not this way. There was a vexing stirring within me—a stirring that left me questioning my very being. The by-products of the stirring were fear and dread. And there were so many other unhealthy emotions and expressions of myself.

That's me and my magic mirror on the wall. How about you? What do you see? What does your mirror say? Do you like what it has been saying?

A couple of years ago, I had the privilege of going through training for life-coach certification, with my mentor. This was a training program that equipped us to coach individuals through various stages in life— mostly the disappointing stages in life. Painful pasts, fear of the future, grief, etc. The program was also fitted to coach ourselves through life and its encumbrances, just as much as we trained to coach others. After all, we could not possibly coach others while keeping our own rubble buried.

One of the exercises we employed during training was called the "primary question." In this exercise, we were asked to do a mental scan our inner selves and uproot any underlying, conflicting questions that we may have unmindfully tucked away in our mind, like sifting our thoughts through a sieve. And what was dredged up from within me were these questions: *What is wrong with me? Why am I so useless?*

Along the span of the process, I realized I had asked myself these questions before. Out loud and in my conscious mind. What I failed to realize up until this point was that these questions had taken seat in my subconscious, occupying real estate in my mind, gearing the wheels of my thinking to doubt my adequacy. I had, unawares to myself, set myself in the ring, for a boxing match between me and unworthiness. The latter was throwing the majority of the punches.

If you would ask yourself, what question may you have posed to yourself. What have you asked yourself, out loud or in musing? Does your question yield a positive, productive response? You need to know that you are worth the time that is committed to unearthing this primary question within you, to filter it out of your mind. Then replace it with another question, an undivided, well-intentioned question that will bring you fruitful answers and take you to a place of powerful productivity for yourself and for others.

If you are the kind of person who feels like hands-on experiences and exercises bring you healing, or if it helps you to chalk mark that line of before healing and after healing, then do so. Write down your negative question on a piece of paper. Now that you have identified the problem question, tear it up, throw it out, and burn it—whatever you think will bring you the convincing that this is behind you. Then write down a good question, a self-motivating line, or a passage of scripture that will inspire you. It would also encourage you further if you penned your good question or scripture on a note card or paper and taped it to your mirror or set it on your dashboard—anywhere that allows you visibility daily.

These are all ways that proved effective for me. There is not a prescribed formula to this. For me, the most valuable aspect of this exercise was the act of being able to benchmark the moment that brought about some transition from my previous state. Seeing the negating thoughts on paper opened my eyes to the content, to recognize what I had corked inside of myself. As I mentioned previously, it does not have to be only the revised primary question that you tape to your mirror. It could be motivational quotes from sources that inspire you.

One of the most compelling notes that I taped to the mirror is the word of God. I was right at the midpoint of my struggle when my pastor once reminded us off the pulpit, about the power of declaring the word. I had heard this recommended various times from other sermons and speakers. But on that day, something my pastor said left an imprint on my heart. He said, "When you are unable to speak the word, *write it down*." This jolted me so, because at this stage, I needed help. I needed hope.

The depression had overturned my health to extreme frailty and incapability in accomplishing anything. I'm not talking about some big feat. I'm talking about my daily chores—cooking, cleaning, sleeping. Every routine I could do without even having to think, became undoable. The physical ailments handed me several days of feebleness that hindered my ability to even speak as I normally would.

This was where what my pastor said proved immensely valuable to me. When I could not open my mouth to utter the promises of the word over my life, I started to *write them down*. And before long, this became my journal. The word filled every page of my journal. The potency of this exercise has been so evident in my life that to this day, I *write down* the "active, operative, energizing and effective" word every day in my journal (Hebrews 4:12 AMPC). The work for our healing has to begin inside-out and the word of God certainly possesses the persuasive power to do this.

And then there were days when just taping scripture to my mirror wouldn't be sufficient. I couldn't possibly stand in front of my mirror during the night. Ironically, I could have because sleep deprivation was beginning to evolve out of my struggle.

This was just one of the other dragging outcomes of depression for me. I stayed awake, wide-eyed for so many nights. I wish I could say it was days, weeks, or months even. I had to inevitably push back against this yoke for over a year and a half. I had never before this had any issues with my sleep routine. It was just fine, until now. Since this was another new one, I didn't know what to do with this for quite some time. I would toss and turn and then flip over again and again.

Now this was not to help me spend my sleepless nights without being bored, but somehow, we decided to get a television for our bedroom. So, my night owl eyes turned to the television screen. This time the purpose indeed was to kill the boredom of insomnia. And bonus, I imagined it might drown out the melancholy. I would watch sitcom reruns back to back. *Everybody Loves Raymond*, *King of Queens*, *Frasier*, and so on—these sitcom characters became my friends through many nights. I figured maybe all the funny would make me feel better.

Unfortunately, it turned out that the funny wasn't

doing what I had expected. And eventually it gave way to solid insomnia. Some unrelenting power it had – this sleeplessness. I wish the actual nights were somewhat as light as they sound—not so much. Several nights were disturbing. Insomnia was now a monster to me. It goes without saying, the countless effects this can have on the body and an already disturbed mind. Night and day became irrelevant to me. Time had turned into one convoluted mess.

At some point later I started to plug-in the word, sermons, and audio Bible into my ears at night. Thank heaven for headphones. My every night now became immersed in the word and the sermons. Depression has the potential to hit harder when we are sleep deprived, especially in the night watch. This turned out to be a great weapon to drown out the oppressive thoughts. If it wasn't going to let down, I decided to drown it out.

Each time we identify ourselves with the word, we are shifting toward conceivably seeing ourselves for who we were created to be. When we look at ourselves in the light of the word, our reflection in the mirror will respond with confidence, and courage, and hope. The word, is our mirror.

> And all of us, as with unveiled face, because we continued to behold in the Word of God, *as in a mirror* the glory of the Lord, are being constantly

transfigured into His very own image in ever increasing splendor and from one degree of glory to another. (2 Corinthians 3:18 AMP)

How great is this! When we look into the word, we are looking into a mirror that unveils our inhibitions and fears. We are looking into a mirror that has the capacity to transform. And when the veil lifts, what is in front of us is a renewed "me." The process of our transformation is ever increasing. It is progressive. Translation, our *me* improves every day, when we keep this mirror before us. Our reflection revolves from the lies we saw in ourselves to a true, unreserved, and glowing reflection. Unveil your depression. Expose the intimidating spirit of depression to the mirror of the word.

I've had several friends tell me that they felt judged and condemned when they read the word. One friend in particular said that she would feel so bad while reading the word that she just had to shut the book and push it away. She refrained from reading the Bible for an extended period. She said she wasn't able to recognize or feel God's love as she read. And deep inside I knew that I was exactly like her at one point. Her expression gave me a glimpse of what my struggle would have looked like, had I been able to step away from myself and watch from the outside in.

My friend is now in such a wonderful place in her

relationship with the Lord. It makes me gleam with joy just watching her. But her struggle was undeniably real. I stepped back and wondered many times about how I could help her through this.

During the times when I was entrenched in condemnation, I would feel it everywhere—at church, in sermons, in songs, in the word. The enemy had used my state of depression to his advantage to get me to brood over and over in my mind, of how unworthy I was. Remember, I used to shy away from my mirror. How was I going to look into the word if I couldn't even look at myself in the mirror?

But I have to confess, what got me over my contention with condemnation, was the word itself. I must stand by the liberating power of the word. The confession, the sticky notes on the mirror, writing it down in my journal, the audio word—all of it. This soaking in of the word was a significant part of my freedom. The word was literally my advocate against the condemnation. The more I absorbed the word, the more I experienced and embraced the love of God. He loved me before I even knew Him. He knew what He was getting when He loved me. My failures and letdowns, do not let my Savior down. And golly, did it take me some mileage to get to this wonderful, freeing truth.

There is no fear in love [dread does not exist], but full-grown (complete, perfect) love turns fear out of doors and expels every trace of terror! For fear brings with it the thought of punishment, and [so] he who is afraid has not reached the full maturity of love [is not yet grown into love's complete perfection]. (1 John 4:18 AMPC)

I had to embrace His love in all its fullness, unfiltered by my thoughts and feelings—feelings of inadequacy and condemnation. And sure enough, gradually and consistently, I was able to look at *me* again—face my *mirror* again. Keep this mirror of the word, on the wall … it will reflect the truth. Why should we fear? Why should we doubt? After all, it was He who loved us first.

We love Him, because He first loved us. (1 John 4:19 AMPC)

CHAPTER 4
Shame

In the darkness. She hides there.
It's shelter, it's safe, it's veiled.
All her fears and wounds she nurses
there.
No one should come close to her
shadow.
None allowed to catch a glimpse of her
eyes.
There's pain there.
There's shame there.
With only one person she lays it bare.
She. Herself.
But she doesn't want to live there.

Remember the woman with the issue of bleeding? She
might as well have walked around with a red X on her
forehead, deeming her unclean, especially because of
the times and culture she lived in. This woman in the

New Testament had been living with a hemorrhage issue for twelve years. She had consulted with and spent all her money on many physicians, only for her illness to get worse.

Jesus happened to be in her vicinity of Galilee, thronged in the midst of a large crowd that obviously wanted a touch of healing from Jesus or simply wanted an opportunity to see this miracle-working celebrity of their time. They were hoping that if they got lucky, they could possibly witness a miracle. Jesus was in fact on His way to operate in another prayer of supernatural healing for a synagogue official's daughter, who was at the verge of death.

That's when Jesus's procession with the crowd was interrupted midpath, by something no one else noticed. But Jesus stopped, and turned around to survey the crowd, looking for the someone He knew had touched Him. He then asked out loud a question that would be translated as ridiculous by his disciples, and even you and me, I'm imagining, if we were there. But Jesus turned around and asked out loud, "Who touched My *clothes*?"

His clothes? How could He possibly feel someone touching His clothes, when He was being pressed in by a crowd? His clothes would have already been very likely touched and pulled and wrinkled quite substantially. But Jesus, He knew that there had been an impartation. A transmission of healing had taken place.

She probably thought she could have sneaked out through the crowd, just as nimbly as she had managed to make her way in to the middle of the crowd. But the woman knew that she had been discovered. As much as she was ashamed to, and as much as it unnerved her, she knew she had to reveal herself. The one whose mere fringe of clothing had the power to arrest her long spell of hemorrhaging, would no doubt be able to reveal her, if He desired. She nervously made herself known, and told Him her story. Her story was one of *shame*.

She had something to hide, and that is why, instead of walking up to Jesus and asking Him to heal her, she came up obscurely behind Him, camouflaged in the crowd, and touched the tassels hanging off the edge of His clothes. The story goes on to convey that Jesus was elated at her outright action of faith. This woman could have lived the illness-packed, ostracized life she lived up until the day she died. But she decided, that it was time to take control of her future by depending on Jesus for her healing.

Wouldn't you say that *depending* and *taking control* are two paradoxical ends? She had to rein in the control of making the decision toward her healing. And at the same time, she had to relinquish control... and depend, on the one that could take her impossibility and turn it around. And so, as the story goes, the shunned woman braved a chance of walking into the middle of a crowd that could have possibly stoned her for polluting them with her uncleanness.

> And He said to her, Daughter, your faith, your trust and confidence in Me, springing from faith in God, has restored you to health. Go in (into) peace and be *continually healed* and *freed* from your, distressing bodily, disease. (Mark 5:34 AMPC)

So why did this woman want to hurriedly grab her healing and tiptoe away unnoticed? If society managed to twine a culture of shame around mental disorders today, in her day and age they were far less tolerant of an illness of the kind she had. Under Mosaic law, a woman with an issue of blood, was rendered unclean and had to maintain separation for seven days. Along with her, anybody who touched her, everything that she slept on and sat on, and anyone who touched anything that she touched was also coupled with her as unclean.

Talk about being stigmatized! To take matters a foot further, any woman who had this discharge prolonged past her regular *unclean* period was considered unclean, as long as she had the issue. All of the above—anybody that touched her and anything that she touched regulation—was carried onto this woman's drawn-out illness as well.

What she touched on Jesus's clothing was the tassels at the edge of His robe. This blue tassel was a requirement in Old Testament law, to be attached to the border of their robes. Every time they look at this tassel, it was to be a reminder to them to be obedient to the commandments of the Lord and to walk in holiness and to recall the history of their miraculous exodus from Egypt (Numbers 15:38–40 AMPC).

The tassels represent the commandments, the word. Could it be that she recognized the healing power of the word, so much that she recognized the authority those tassels carried?

Here are some takeaways from the woman's story. As per Mosaic law, anything and anyone the woman touched was coded as unclean. The unclean person had to then bathe and wash his or her clothes, and he or she would continue to be unclean until sundown. Wouldn't Jesus fall in the unclean category now? His clothes had been touched by this unclean woman—a woman who, in all probability, would be avoided by everyone. After all, who would want to have to wash and rewash their clothes and stay blacklisted from the community until dusk?

I wonder at times, how she made it through the crowd without being discovered. After Jesus brought her out front, I'm imagining it would have been a spectacle there with people scrambling out of there to go home and wash themselves clean. Shame was inscribed into their law and invariably into their culture.

Jesus was aware of the law and didn't hesitate to reveal her, and affirm His authority over her healing. I think He had to reveal her, or else no one would have believed that the unclean woman had become clean overnight. Even after walking away with physical healing, she would have had to continue her shame walk. Jesus helped her walk away, untainted from the shame.

She would have had an awkward dilemma on her hands if she wasn't able to evidence her healing or if no one had believed her because, that's who she was for a very long time. The unclean woman. He may have embarrassed her momentarily, but Jesus called her forward to undo the shame that had her entangled. He wanted her to be a testimony of freedom from the shame. The weightier issue here wasn't the bleeding; it was the shame.

I was ashamed for a good part of the life of my depression. Me, you, and many others are hiding in the dark, trying to conceal ourselves among a crowd. Sometimes we hide, and sometimes we run. And that's where the devil has his party. As long as he has you ashamed and shadowed in the dark, he's got the upper hand. "People think you are being fake. People think it's all in your head. You go out there, and people are going to start criticizing you. It's best if no one knows." Do any of these sound remotely familiar? They are lies that hold you back in shame.

However, just like the woman in our narrative,

Christ is calling you and me out to walk out of our shame, to expose the deception of shame, and to undo the twine, which society has woven into the fabric of mental illness.

We end up being so troubled about what people may think or what they may say. And oftentimes our concern is valid. Some people simply don't understand. I have been told by the people that I needed to "get over it" or that I needed to "eat more." It was hard to swallow these unmindful suggestions. I was expected to get over my illness at their suggested prescriptions. And I'm not referring to medicinal prescriptions here. Of course I wanted to get over it. I had two babies to mother, and I clearly could not afford to stay down at will.

I have a turtleneck sweater analogy to explain this feeling of suffocation. If you are claustrophobic, like I am, you can probably relate. I would say it was like putting your head into the neck of a turtleneck sweater. You put your head through the neck of the sweater, and you are stuck. You are suffocating and straining to get your head out of the constraints of the sweater neck. It was just as suffocating to withstand the comments and opinions. And so, I would resist sharing my struggle with depression.

I didn't share again with anyone, until I started spiraling further down into chronic depression. My husband and I had to open up to a handful of close confidants. Some of these are still close friends and mentors to this day. We treasure these friendships dearly. Then there were some others who didn't want to be a source of support but rather preferred to dish out their opinions. They may lend an ear but eventually do more damage than care. Be careful about who knows your story, especially when you are smack down in the center of the struggle. One careless word will suffice to send you further into deep rejection.

I did not need that to accompany the sense of abandonment and solitude that already shadowed alongside me every day. Once I was able to pass the hiding phase I talked about in the hiding place chapter, I made attempts to step outside and take myself for a spin around the community. I pulled through these better than I expected of myself. But here arose a perplexity to my mode of surviving depression.

The woman in our story took on a "hiding herself" and "keeping herself obscure" survival method. While I, dressed up my everyday with a façade of smiles, masked busyness, and simulated excitement. And then I wondered why no one seemed to care about my struggle. They passed by me, happy, dressed up, and looking well. Didn't they care?

Here's when I had the spotlight turned on me. The question was on me. What was I doing? If I was keeping my pain masked so well, how would they know? This was a lot of extra, backstage pretend work I had going on, flanking with the already painful contractions of depression. Little did I know that there were many backstage workers with me, concealed behind the veil. A group of people I did not know existed, masking their pain just as convincingly as I did. You see, the woman with the bleeding issue, and me with the depression, and you, we are all trying to adapt to the shame. We just have our own discrete angles to the mode of adaptation.

The woman was obviously so depleted from living with the pain of the shame that she just had to run to her chance, through this crowd that was dense enough that she could probably slip through unnoticed. There's that kind of running. And then there's the kind of running that is opted for more as an escape, much like the one I took on.

Have you felt like you just wanted to run too—run from the depression, run from the pain? Have you felt like running away from *you*? I have wanted to and did so, as I shared earlier in chapter 1 about my middle of the night running episodes. I would pick up and run, on impulse. I did not know what I was running from. I just knew I needed to get away.

I now realize that I was running away from whatever was tormenting me. Only when my husband drove around in the night, with two babies in the backseat, found me, and took me home, the torment came back home with me. When the running was exhausted, I hid in the dark of my closet, under my clothes. Desperately, screaming into a pillow to muffle the sound, yearning for all this to pass. It was terribly painful to live with myself, with the depression, the pain, the shame! More often than not, where there's depression, there is shame. But depression and shame, do not have to go hand in hand.

If Jesus could call out the stigma of shame in His day, we can too. The woman with the issue dealt with shame. You and I, undeniably deal with shame. Hannah also had to deal with shame. She was a woman drooping from the shame and anguish of being barren. She was being bitterly provoked and embarrassed of her plight. During one of her visits to the temple of the Lord, she was weeping and pouring out her heart before God. It was in so much anguish that Eli, the temple priest, assumed she was drunk and rebuked her.

> But Hannah answered, "No, my lord, I am a woman with a despairing spirit. I have not been drinking wine or any intoxicating drink, but I have poured out my soul before the LORD ... I have spoken until now out of my great concern and [bitter] provocation." (1 Samuel 1:15–16 AMP)

Hannah poured out her sorrow, her complaint. She poured out her shame. It had all been exposed. And it goes on to say in the same chapter, after all that pouring out, that she returned home and *her face was no longer sad.*

It may seem like we are at the eleventh hour for a chance of redemption from this shame. But it is not a chance bygone. As the hand keeps ticking on the clock of mental illness, the hour has come to rend the veil of shame, canopying over this illness. The reason I ventured out to share my story is for you who are enclosed in the darkness of shame. You need to know that you are not alone. You don't have to be ashamed of your wounds. You will feel shame. But you do not have to take residence there.

The pain is real. The symptoms are real, just as real as they are in any other illness. If you and I can talk about the illnesses that make our bodies take a plunge, we should be able to do the same with illnesses that grapple our minds.

I used to be ashamed. I am not ashamed of my struggle with depression anymore. I am now only ashamed … of my shame.

CHAPTER 5
Good Pain

The best way out is always through.
—Robert Frost

Okay. So you are standing up to your battle with depression. You've confronted it. You've revealed it. You're not hiding anymore. You've told the people in your life that you struggle with mental illness. What's next?

Here is where we are going to possibly challenge ourselves the most during the duration of the depression. If we could step outside of ourselves for a few moments. If we could lend ourselves to ease the heartache of another—that is, if our bodies permit us the health and liberty to do so. Then, we should make a sincere effort to reach out to someone else who may be struggling like us, possibly struggling more than you and I did.

It is not going to be easy. It is a decision that

requires a whole lot of prayer. Ask for counsel from those who love you and have been steadily supporting you during your spar with depression. Consult with yourself, and see if your health will permit this. There are a lot of factors to consider. And this endeavor may have the potential to be painful, or at the least uncomfortable.

I know, you're thinking, *What is the point of reading on if all you are going to tell me is, here's an idea for more pain that you can have on top of all the pain I already endure?* Right? All I'm asking is that you trek with me, and I will explain, in the best possible way, how this worked out in my journey with depression.

Keep in mind that I could not always do this. I could not always step out, serve, or reach out to others as I had hoped. As I mentioned earlier, the physical challenges I had to encounter, along with the depression, were several. A few months after the diagnosis with postpartum depression, I developed shingles. If you have already been through this, I am able to sincerely empathize with you. If you haven't, I hope you never experience this. Needless to say, it is painful! With my newborn baby and toddler, and with not much help to gather, I was able to grant them both the gift of chicken pox.

Almost immediately after I recovered from this illness, I started to notice that I was having trouble moving around like I normally would. There was no way I could stay down at will because I had my children and other responsibilities around the house. In addition to this, I was in my final semester of graduate school. In other words, I had a lot to do and a lot of movement to accomplish all the to-dos. However, before I knew it, I was unable to get out of bed. In addition to that, I was unable to even shift myself around in bed. And little by little I was confined to the bed and almost entirely immobilized. It was perpetual pain all over my body. Of course, this drove us to the doctor—or doctors, I should say. And this was where I was diagnosed with the fibromyalgia.

I had never even heard of the disorder before. Fibromyalgia is sometimes triggered by some forms of physical trauma. And in other cases, the trigger could be psychological stress. In my case, it was a result of both. I had to have surgery for my back a few weeks before all these other symptoms evolved. The result—chronic pain all over their body, alongside fatigue and sleeplessness. So if you struggle with unexplainable pain along with the depression, it may be worth a visit to the doctor.

The reason I am laying out some of these physical symptoms, along with the suggestion to entrust yourself to serve others, is to make you aware of the importance of listening to your body and taking care of yourself. I didn't respond the way I should have to the chronic pain in my body. In attempting to be as benevolent as I could, I thought gulping down prescription pain killers and putting myself on the line to serve others was a good cause, worth the pain. I plead with you not to do the same. Your physical health should take precedence, along with your mental health.

Now, rerouting this monologue to the idea of serving while you are still in your struggle. In my situation, I grasped this truth—the more I gave of myself to others in service, the more I could take my mind off of my struggle with depression. I am aware that the practicality of this notion may not be feasible for everyone and in every circumstance. But it felt like it was worth enduring the *good pain* to counter the *bad pain.*

David Vobora is the founder of the Adaptive Training Foundation. He was once speaking at my home church. And during his message, he talked about using good pain to push out bad pain. David Vobora, a former NFL athlete (with the St. Louis Rams 2008–2010 and Seattle Seahawks 2010–2011), was inspired to start a gym for people who were permanently disabled. His vision includes working especially with the veteran community. He works with each individual by equipping and propelling him or her to reengage in fitness and health activities through customized adaptive performance training. He motivates athletes who have sustained life-altering injuries to see past and push past their physical limitations, and he takes them to a level of training and performance that rational and logical thinking would regard as insurmountable.

You would have to see it to grasp how these amazing individuals override daring training feats, making them appear nothing short of extraordinary. In other words, these amazing individuals are empowered to brace themselves and brave the good pain to push out the bad pain that resulted from their permanent limitations. The bad pain—that is the result of the disability. The good pain is the result of using will and strength to push past the bad pain.

This extraordinary idea of engaging and braving good pain to push out the bad pain resonated powerfully within me. I came across David's motivating principle only recently. But he puts it in perfectly accurate words that I could not have explained while I was in the process of serving others through my pain. When he said this from the pulpit that day, all I could think of was how liberated I felt, as I had started to reach out to others even as I was still swallowing my own pill of pain and depression. Even though it took more effort than it normally would, even though I had to step aside—not push aside but rather step aside—from my pain for a little while, there was freedom in it for me.

I am not saying that I was entirely free, but each step I took to reach others brought gradual but undeniable freedom. Rest assured—it was working. Healing was beginning to unfold. It was worth enduring every bit of emotional pain I may have had to undergo, even as I reached out to others who were hurting. There is a release, a freedom, that emanates from this kind of self-giving that isn't readily explainable, and yet it is liberating.

A freedom that tells you it is all right to be weak for a season because there is an incremental strength that you accumulate from letting God be strong for you during your weakness.

> I was given the gift of a handicap to keep me in constant touch with my limitations. Satan's angel did his best to get me down; what he in fact did was push me to my knees. No danger then of walking around high and mighty! At first I didn't think of it as a gift, and begged God to remove it. Three times I did that, and then he told me, My grace is enough; it's all you need. My strength comes into its own in your weakness. Once I heard that, I was glad to let it happen. I quit focusing on the handicap and began appreciating the gift. It was a case of Christ's strength moving in on my weakness. Now I take limitations in stride, and with good cheer, these limitations that cut me down to size—abuse, accidents, opposition, bad breaks. I just let Christ take over! And so the weaker I get, the stronger I become. (2 Corinthians 12:7–10 MSG)

These are the words of the apostle Paul in his letter to the church of the Corinthians, the man who authored most of the New Testament. He was willing to send his weakness in the direction of a greater destiny—a greatness and destiny that could only culminate when he placed his weakness into the arms of the strength of Christ. He allowed the strength of Christ to be a canopy over him, to "pitch a tent over and dwell upon me" (2 Corinthians 12:9 AMPC).

Paul asked the Lord three times for this pain or handicap to be taken away. I think Paul was being patient. I asked—not just three times but rather countless number of times. "Take this away from me," I said … a lot! Paul's "thorn in the flesh"—we don't know if it was a physical ailment, a mental issue, or an emotional challenge perhaps. Sometimes God allows some events in our lives to linger longer than we care to have them. So that, when we eventually get our victories, we realize, "Wow, that wasn't me. I would have never survived all that on my own. That there was a supernatural factor, the hand of God, that brought me out."

Perhaps it was in His plan for me to record my journey in this way, a journey that evolved because something caused me so much pain. My eyes were opened to see how God sustained me through the hardness of this journey. And He, put this passion in my heart to reach out to those who are hurting like I did, to assure you that you can do it too—to tell you that one day, the seeming impossibility of this journey will fade away. That even as I retrace for you every step of the sting of my journey, you are able to so closely relate to this as you read and say, "God, that's me!" Or, You could also read the hopeful half of this book and one day be able to say, "That's me too! That could be my story. Or that *is* my story."

If there is ever a piece of literature in the pages of history, that demonstrates the tremendous purpose and overriding power that comes from serving through pain, it is in *The Hiding Place.* Corrie Ten Boom paints a painstakingly powerful picture of the trenches she and her family were thrown into and gives us a remarkable account of the service they selflessly gave out to war-worn, lost people.

There in her book, in between all the harshness of the calamities of war, she talks about a simpler form of service. She talks about a servant heart that served through strengths and even through disabilities—her mother, Cornelia Ten Boom. Cornelia lived in service to the poor and suffering around her. Cooking meals and gifting warm visits to those in pain was her stirring. At one point in her biography, Corrie provides an account of the life-altering illness that pulled her mother away from living an able life.

One afternoon at her kitchen sink, Corrie found her mother slowly collapsing and caving into the cerebral hemorrhage that had captured her body. It led to her being paralyzed from hand to foot, and she slipped into a coma. Although she never entirely recovered enough to reach her serving capacity, she was able to regain consciousness and movement to hold her own. She lost her speech capabilities and could only motion with her eyes to communicate an object or a desire she had.

Mrs. Cornelia Ten Boom was now seated by the window at their home they called the Beje. And every time she saw someone pass by and she remembered their birthday, she would motion with the limited physical capabilities she had. She would have Corrie write a little note, wishing that person and telling him or her that she had seen him or her from the window. She managed to sign every note with her stiffened fingers, in handwriting that may have been scrawly, but in every curve of her writing, there was love.

She was previously able to take her love out the door with her soup pots and sewing baskets. But Corrie says of her mother, "But now that these things were taken away, the love seemed as whole as before. She sat in her chair at the window and loved us. She loved the people she saw in the street—and beyond: her love took in the city..."

And Miss Corrie Ten Boom brings it all together in this sentence:

> "And so I learned that love is larger than the walls that shut it in."   - Corrie Ten Boom

This is a decision that would have to be made with determination and purpose in mind. And bear in mind, you may not be able to accomplish every task you purpose in your heart. I think one should allow oneself some grace for that. Direct focus toward a service, a cause that speaks to your heart. It may be to simply step out and be willing to lend an ear, or shoulder the pain of another depression-stricken person like you. It may be to serve in a soup kitchen or homeless shelter.

I began to step out and do these things. Please do understand that I am not saying these things like I was functioning from a place of confidence, strength, and a sound mind. No, the struggle was still as clear as daylight. I was still weak, still in pain. But when I started to speak with other women who struggled like me, I could sympathize with them and see them from a place of absolute understanding. I didn't have to try hard to comprehend their pain. It was as real to me as it was to them. Yes, the degree of suffering varies from one person to the other. Nevertheless, the capacity to identify with one another was of one accord.

Healing from the mental malady of depression could come from several places. For some it may be the medicines, the treatment they receive from their psychiatrists, through miracles, through prayer. The passageways are many. In my case, one of the avenues of my stride toward freedom was in stepping out of my pain and being willing to step into another's pain. It helped me to see that I was not the only one. I believe it is common for those of us battling depression to have the misconstrued notion that we are alone. We are positively not alone. But stepping out of myself enabled me to take all attention off myself.

My isolated, inward living was preoccupied with nursing my own wounds and wallowing in self-pity - which is all right for a season. I truly believe that. It is all right to allow our mind to release the pain through the healthy emotions God has gifted to us. But the season cannot and should not be unending. At some point we have to try and mark that sentence with a period and move on to the next sentence in our story.

At this point, I wasn't depression free, but I was beginning to taste morsels of the freedom. The life-impeding fear had been dealt with at this stage, primarily through undergoing life-coaching exercises with my mentor. If you are allowed a chance at this kind of coaching, please, avail yourself of the opportunity. I had known before I started to step out of my cocoon that I was being called to share my story while the struggle was still alive. I would ponder within, *Who would possibly care to hear tales of pain and suffering?* People want the epic stories, the stories of the overcomer, or so I thought. I told myself habitually that I had nothing to offer to anyone.

Through the span of time, I learned otherwise. I learned that when there is a calling on our lives, and we are living in communication and obedience to God, the calling will follow us wherever we go. First thing in the morning, last thing before bed, while cooking, while driving, it pursues you. It doesn't nag. Rather, it instigates a passion, a yearning that something is incomplete in you. There is more you need to do with your life.

On one occasion, when the calling was still beckoning to me, we happened to have a rather sizable women's event at my church. It was a night filled with fun, excitement, and powerful testimonies. I was seated in the dark of the crowd, right between my good friends. Again, this was my home church, so there were many women I was friends with in the audience. But it didn't matter how many friends there were; I felt lonely. I felt like I was alone and ignored, and like no one cared. I wanted to leave.

Somehow, I made it through the evening. Bedtime was beaten by this feeling of abandonment and loneliness. I sat up in bed, crying all night, asking God to relieve me of this feeling. The crying and pleading extended to dawn, when around five in the morning, I had a heavy, powerful impression on my heart that I needed to come out with my story. There were many in the dark who were feeling isolated like I did, who needed to know they were not alone. This time, rather than just following me, the calling stuck.

I still wasn't able to take that step, until my loving friend Martha, who was always my support during this time, announced to a group of women that I would start a group. She had taken the first step for me, just like God had Aaron head start the mission to deliver the people of Israel from bondage in Egypt, because Moses was hesitant to go. Moses listed out his speech impediment, his lack of leadership skills, and his fear and laid them out before God. That's when God told Aaron to go ahead and do the part. Well, I too listed my inadequacies before God. Moses did eventually obey God and lead the nation out of Egypt. Eventually, I obeyed too and started a group.

I told my story. I took out the punctuations and periods. I shared it all. Slowly, a small crowd of women began their exodus from the dark. They began sharing with me their personal struggles with depression. I was shocked beyond words. Here was an illiterate me, assuming that I was alone, that nobody would benefit from hearing my story of brokenness. I was wrong. Some of those women have become the tightest, closest bunch of friends to me today.

It was just a conversation over coffee my friend Aubree and I were having. The topic being depression because we had both battled it. One thing she said echoed within me. We were talking about how there's not enough support groups or active dialogue about depression in most churches. And I, for one, had constantly been praying and waiting for the day when I would have it all together and then be able to share my testimony of deliverance with others. And that's when Aubree said, "I am so glad you shared your testimony when you did. It made me realize that I was not crazy or alone. I am tired of seeing the women on platforms who have it all together. Where are the real struggles? You shared the real struggle, and that is what I needed to hear."

That has stuck with me since then. What Aubree said made me realize that it is during the journey through depression that we need to hear that there are others out there just like us. That it is not all in our heads. Doubtless we need the testimonies of victory indeed. How else can we point people to hope? I myself have been personally inspired by the powerful testimonies of several women. But the testimonies of the *raw struggle* are every bit as valuable.

There are people out there that are in the shadows just like you and I. They need to know we are out there too. Let your story be their release from the imprisonment of depression. Allow yourself some good pain. As hard as it is do, steward your pain. Steer it toward the benefit of others. You could be the answer to someone else's pain.

> So let's not allow ourselves to get fatigued doing good. At the right time we will harvest a good crop if we don't give up, or quit. Right now, therefore, every time we get the chance, let us work for the benefit of all, starting with the people closest to us in the community of faith. (Galatians 6:9–10 MSG)

CHAPTER 6
Your Pain for Gain

Elijah was a man with a nature like ours.
—James 5:17 AMP

Who was Elijah? When we hear the name Elijah, most of us are reminded of the mighty prophet of God, who called down fire from heaven with one audacious prayer. He outran a king's chariot on his own two legs. He was transported up to heaven in a whirlwind. He had supernatural experiences on earth that most of us may never be privileged to witness in our lifetime. He was a man who left behind a legacy of power.

Hence, doesn't it sound widely contrasting when Elijah is called "a man with a nature like ours"? According to James, in his New Testament letter to the church, "Elijah was a man with a nature like ours, with the same physical, mental and spiritual limitations and shortcomings" (James 5:17 AMP). Wow! Take that in for a while.

Often, we identify people with their strengths and accomplishments. What was the first thought that came to your mind when you read the name Elijah? Chances are you were reminded of the miracles he performed and the immense boldness he displayed during his time on earth. We have that tendency to associate the heroes of faith with their triumphs rather than their trials.

But I think when James referred to Elijah as "a man with a nature like ours," he was beckoning us to relate not just with this prophet's strengths. He was also pointing us to his weaknesses, just as much as his strength. When he asks us to pray like Elijah, who commanded and arrested the elements of nature with his prayer, there was a degree of comparison he was also drawing to this man who ran away and hid himself in a cave, in fear. That this was a man with a weak nature, just as ours.

It is worth a visit to Elijah's single-handed performance on Mount Carmel to comprehend this. The prophet poses a brazen challenge to the prophets of the pagan god Baal—Elijah versus 450 prophets of Baal. The battle was a sacrifice, and the challenge was to determine who had the sacrifice that would summon the showmanship of their respective gods. They choose an ox each to place on the altar with wood. And the challenge was that they could not kindle the fire themselves. The fire had to be kindled by either one of their gods.

The Baalites got their turn first. They called, cried, and danced to Baal from morning to noon. Elijah went as far as mocking and asking them to cry louder just in case their god was asleep. Then, possibly provoked by the mocking, the prophets made a dramatic move and started to cut themselves and let themselves bleed to get the attention of their god. Nothing.

Elijah was up next. He set up the altar, placed the wood and ox on it, and proceeded to dig a trench around the altar. He had four pots of water poured over the sacrifice, three times. It was enough water to run over the sacrifice and flow down to fill the trenches he dug. Finally, he did his thing. He called on the name of the living God. In no time, fire descended from the heavens, consumed the sacrifice, the wood, and the stone altar, and also licked up the water in the trenches. Dry. After this exploit, Elijah had the 450 prophets of Baal seized and slain.

Right after this, the prophet even outran the king's horse chariots by a distance of nearly twenty miles. Now, the news of his expedition reached the queen, who vowed in anger to take his life. Elijah was now afraid. At the queen's threat, he ran for his life on his two legs, a day's journey into the wilderness. His next prayer request to God was to take his life. God sent the angel catering service to feed the depressed Elijah, twice, and he journeyed forty days from just the sustenance of those two meals.

Depressed Elijah then proceeded to hide in a cave.

From mountaintop to cave, God now wanted to know what His powerful prophet was doing here. Elijah responded with despair. He recounted his zealous works for the Lord and then cried for his life. One more time, God asked him the same question: "What are you doing here, Elijah?" Elijah's response hadn't changed. The next word from God to Elijah was asking him to get up and go anoint Elisha as prophet, in his place.

There are two impressions we can take away from this. Our weakness does not have to stop us from accomplishing great things. God knew Elijah's weaknesses before he chose him to be his prophet. Yet He did great works through this one man. We may feel like depression is holding us back. Nevertheless, it is all right to step out in weakness. You, me, Elijah, we are all alike. We're all real people, we're all found wanting in some way. Yet that doesn't stop God from doing great works through us, even in our weakness.

And the other lesson we can take away from Elijah is found in the depression he faced. He cried, feared, and despaired. And God allowed that. But what God did not favor was Elijah nesting there. He permits mourning for a season, but He does not want us to remain in that state. We will never know how much more Elijah could have possibly accomplished if he had stepped out even in his depressed state. He would probably still be the same Elijah—probably still sad and still depressed, but that's okay. All God needed was Elijah—not Elijah's courage or Elijah's strength, just Elijah.

Your weakness, my weakness, is all right by God. It is all right to render our fears and sorrows to a season of release. We should not, however, let it take over our life.

Healing can come even from our struggle. When we struggle, we most definitely desire freedom. We hope to be free and not hurt from it anymore. However, there is a healing that can come from the struggle, by walking in freedom even through the season of pain. As much as it hurts, if we could withstand the pain and use our pain to be an honest story of the raw struggle, there builds up a testimony of healing for others and in the process a greater degree of healing for us.

It would be remarkable if we were healed instantly. Everyone wants that. That may bandage the pain temporarily. But when the next struggle arises, and it usually does, because that's just part of the growing pains in life, we would end up needing more bandages.

The healing is in the growing. The instant healing may make the pain go away but leaves us lacking in strength for whatever other challenges we may have to encounter. Genuine healing happens when we can endure the pain and grow, while enduring the pain. In doing so, we are schooled well for facing any forthcoming encounters. Plus, we are able to come to the valuable aid of hurting masses or individuals.

I am so privileged to have friends who are exemplars

of stewarding the pains they battle and endure. They are hurting, downright hurting, but they display such strength in the middle of that, and what is honorable to witness is the service they render to others, even while they are still in the hurting stage. Cameron was one such friend. She has had to parent a teenage son who had to strive against bipolar depression for over three years. The ongoing challenges for her son have been manic depression and withdrawing from family and friends, among many other chronic symptoms. I have seen her weep till she was red in the face. She has had intervals where she had to withdraw herself from people and just grieve.

However, she never stayed there. She allowed herself a healthy amount of time to process the pain. Then she stood right back up—still hurting, let me remind you. But for every single decline her son took, she responded by presenting herself in selfless service to others.

During one specific period, her son had to be hospitalized. This hurting mother decided to put her pain to the purpose of helping others. One morning she decided to get to her workplace thirty minutes early, with the intention of looking for a person, or persons, who may be hurting. Her desire was to offer them comfort and prayers. She happened to walk by a residential clinic that morning. She saw two mothers standing outside the clinic entrance, visibly sorrowing. Cameron knew inside of her that these two mothers were not there by accident. They were there because of her prayers, to find hurting souls she could openheartedly console. She walked up to the mothers and engaged them in conversation. Both mothers disclosed their anguish about their respective children, who were both battling mental illness and had been admitted to the clinic behind them.

Cameron shared her son's story with these heartbroken mothers, and then offered to pray with them. Before long, all three mothers huddled together hand-in-hand, and Cameron prayed over the mothers and their children. The two mothers hugged her and walked away, comforted and assured that if Cameron, whose son's symptoms were significantly higher, could walk in such fortified freedom, then so could they. No pain is wasted when we yield the pain into the hands of the one who provides restoration to us, and through us, to a larger hurting population.

You may be thinking, *Isn't it fake or simulated when we try to venture out in our weakness and attempt to be strong for someone else?* That argument is not without validity. I tried to serve at homeless shelters and in some other capacities, when I was still pretty much debilitated from the repercussions of the depression. And in all honesty, it did wear me out at times. And like I said in the "Good Pain" chapter, your physical health should take precedence along with your mental health.

But what if we were to work out of pretense? What if we were to put on strength long enough for it to become a natural ability to us? If you would, indulge me here. If the Beast, from the fairy tale *Beauty and the Beast*, despite his animalistic, inhuman exterior, could replicate and adopt human conduct. And he did this long enough to where a kiss transformed his beastly exterior to that of a human. It was as though, with every aspect of human nature he conformed to, he was being progressively transformed into an actual human. I speak from a fairy tale, I know. But what if we try long enough, taking subtle, reflective steps toward this, and observe the adopted, purposeful behavior to translate to our natural disposition?

In his book *Mere Christianity*, C. S. Lewis talks about *good pretense*. He refers to a good kind of pretense, the kind where the "pretense leads up to the real thing."

> When you are not feeling particularly friendly but know you ought to, the best thing you can do, very often, is to put on a friendly manner and behave as if you were a nicer person than you actually are. And in a few minutes, as we all have noticed you will be really feeling friendlier than you were. Very often the only way to get a quality in reality is to start behaving as if you had it already.
> - C.S. Lewis

I am convinced. Like they say, practice makes perfect. Think about it. If you would … give this proposition some "Selah" time.

Small steps is all it requires. Small beginnings. When babies take their initial steps, their steps are small and clumsy. And slowly we watch them go from their ducky, wobbly walks, to taking big strides and eventually running towards what they want. If an injury causes someone to lose the strength and functionality of their legs, the only way to gain that strength back is taking small steps until there is confidence built and then come the larger strides.

No step is too small, if we have our heart and our commitment and God to back it up. Every sizable church or organization we see today did not start that way. It was preceded by the vision in the heart of one person and maybe a handful of people as pillars of support. The word tells us,

"Do not despise these small beginnings"
(Zechariah 4:10 NLT)

My struggle was battling with the thoughts of not being ready enough or considering myself not qualified enough. And with each excuse I made for my ineligibility, I lost precious time. We will never be perfectly ready for anything. Mother Teresa took her step toward mission work as a young girl. Even after she took her final vows of being wholly in the service of the Lord, she knew she had to go further. The sisters were not allowed to leave the enclosures of the convent wall. And yet the poverty outside that wall beckoned her, and she obeyed. And from there evolved the Mother Teresa we know today.

We could venture out to do our part and God will add to it the rest. Getting up from depression is in some measure relative to getting up from a bodily injury. It takes time, it takes persistence and ultimately relying on the father above to lead the way.

When we realize that the capacity to impact a person's life could possibly be in our hands, it could, it should, motivate us to action. If not for everyone you know that is struggling, at the least for one. "What can I do to make a difference?" We may think. We could pin it on our inability to do anything or onto our busy lives, or other inconveniences. We may move on, thinking that someone else is probably already doing it. Or, it could just be a relinquishing thought of "it is too late."

It is never too late. If there is a person in your life, that's been missing in action, check on him or her. Our call, or text, or visit could be the difference between her or him, deciding to give staying alive another chance. You and I could be the difference that withholds a young mother from taking her life. We could be the bridge that allows her kids to have their mommy and cherish her hugs for some more years. We could be the difference... for one.

> "To ease another's heartache is to forget one's own"
>
> Abraham Lincoln

CHAPTER 7
What I See

I am not moved by what I see, I am not moved by
what I feel, I am moved only by what I believe.
—Smith Wigglesworth

Remember Much-Afraid what you have
seen before the mist blotted it out. Never
doubt that the High places are there
towering above you and be quite sure
that what ever happens I mean to bring
you up there exactly as I have promised.
King touched her lips with burning
coal from the altar … burning flame
too beautiful and too horrible to bear.
She lost consciousness. When she
recovered she found that the shepherd
was carrying her in his arms. - Hannah
Hurnard

This was me. I was *Much-Afraid.* When my life got suddenly blotted out by the mist of the clouds of depression, I lost sight of what was beyond the mist. I felt like the God I had trusted all my life had vanished amid the cloud of pain.

The excerpt above is from *Hinds Feet on High Places*, by Hannah Hurnard. This is an allegorical story of the journey of a woman named Much-Afraid. It might as well have been my name, because that's exactly who and what I was—Much-Afraid. My friend Julia gave me this book when she heard me share a bit of my testimony at a small gathering. She had no idea that the book she had just placed in my hands had my name on it, and neither did I.

It is awe-inspiring how God finds little deeds, nice friends, or a complete stranger sometimes to bring you tiny yet timely, tender reminders, just to let you know that he hasn't forgotten you. You know, I did not embrace it or envision it that way at that time. But as they say, later realization is better than never.

Much-Afraid is taking flight from her *Fearing* family, and her abode in the Valley of Humiliation. The journey takes her through several detours, through the desert, the shore of loneliness, and a valley. All along her travel companions are Sorrow and Suffering. Much-Afraid is following the voice of the Chief Shepherd. She comes to many points in her travel where she is unable to climb the heights. On the contrary, she finds herself not making progress and going further down into the valley. From the valley, she ends up at the Shore of Loneliness, with Sorrow and Suffering still by her side. They were faithful companions. And even as her journey seemed to take her lower and farther from her destination, she is being pursued by her unpleasant relatives, Bitterness, Resentment, and Craven Fear. All were trailing after her to take her back to her family that terrifies her, the Fearings.

I don't know about you, but these were all the *relatives* who were pursuing me as I attempted to escape the Valley of Depression. I speak allegorically, no doubt. But like I said, the handing over of this book by my friend could not have been more timely. As I fought off each and every one of those relatives off my back, I had to remind myself of the high places that my Shepherd had promised me, like he had promised Much-Afraid.

And like Much-Afraid, I would lose consciousness. I fainted multiple times during my struggle. Mostly, I would faint from overwhelming fear and despair. And the fainting was frequent. I am not exaggerating here by any means. This happened continually. And then I realized that there was a safe place for me to faint, and to lose consciousness. A place of surrender. Not in surrender to fear or dread. Or the others. But that, I could lose consciousness in the arms of the Shepherd, and He would drive back the vindictive relatives. All along, reminding myself to envision the High places the Savior had promised me.

Do these sound like your relatives from the Valley of Depression? There are the relatives, then there are the giants, and then there's the *me* we talked about earlier, that you see in the mirror. It's the *me* that, in all likelihood, you didn't care for much. And that is no fault of yours. That is a symptom that depression permits into our lives.

God desires for us to look beyond our relatives and giants. He desires for us to enlarge our vision. Let's weigh in the story of Abram and Sara. They had a problem—a vexing problem that would cause most couples to be downhearted: being without child. Abram and Sara were in this depressed state. Their problem was not just barrenness. They were both well-aged—up in the higher end of the decades of life.

Abram's concern was genuine, wouldn't you say? He had no offspring. More importantly, he was given a stupendous promise. God had told him that he would make Abram into a great nation. And here he was, impoverished of let alone a nation, he had not one offspring to kick-start that nation. And then there was his age and Sara's age. They had both long passed the thresholds of biology with regard to a child.

During the course of his waiting, Abram was inside his tent one night conversing with God about leaving his fortune to his servant Eliezer, because of the lack of an heir to whom he could bequeath all his wealth. God gently asked Abram to step outside of his tent. Abram did so. He pointed Abram to the night sky and asked him to count the stars and promised him descendants as innumerable as the stars.

Do you see what unfolded here? God needed Abram to *step out of his tent* and take in the stars and vastness of the sky to comprehend the vastness of His promise. We attempt to understand God's promises within the constrained limits of our circumstances. Anything past that is beyond our understanding. That is precisely how we know the promise is truly from God. God's promises are impossible for man. His promises are possible only through Him

> For however many promises God has made, they all find their "Yes" in connection with him; that is why it is through him that we say the " Amen " when we give glory to God. (2 Corinthians 1:20 CJB)

Inside his tent, Abram would look at his wife and his mirror, in which he would in all likelihood study his own reflection … and frown. All the disappointments he looked at inside his tent stood in the way of his faith. God had to pull Abram out of that tent to change his perspective.

Sometimes God allows things or events in our lives to extend a little longer than we would have liked—maybe a whole lot longer than we would have liked—so that, just like Much-Afraid, when we eventually walk out of it, we will turn back and know, "That wasn't me. There is no way I would have made it out of that myself." You realize that there was unquestionably a supernatural factor that brought you out, that carried you in his arms.

I stayed in my tent for a very long time. The mirrors reminded me of my failures and weakness. The depression told me I should isolate myself because I am not presentable to the outside world. It portrayed the outside world as a frightful place. My safety would be staying home, in seclusion.

I believe God wanted me to step out of my tent, to gather a larger vision, a perspective that was beyond me, to look at the stars and know that His promise to me is greater than I can even begin to try to imagine or achieve. I also believe that He wanted me to step out, take my eyes off of me, and see the wider audience—to envision a multitude that is braving yet another day with depression on their shoulders. An audience as vast as the stars needs to hear about the honest weaknesses and burdens of a depression survivor. That does not include just my story but your story. They need to hear about the God who takes our disabled past or present and turns it into a future of potential.

If the story of the stars does not suffice in inspiring you, we could look at the story of the grasshoppers. Don't worry, I am not about to venture into a study of the science, or anatomy of grasshoppers. Where we are glancing into is the story of Caleb and the leaders of the twelve tribes of Israel. They were standing at the threshold of crossing into the promised land of Canaan. Moses sent these men out to explore the land and figure out the layout to study the productivity of the land before they cross the border and take possession.

The scouting men returned with the analytics report that Moses had required of them. Also as evidence, they carried back a single cluster of grapes that was so large that it had to be carried by two men, on a pole between them. It was confirmed that they would never lack for good food in the new land, not to leave out grapes.

But they saw problems amid the plethora of fruit. The problem was the people living there. They were powerful, their cities were strong, and there were even giants in the land. Even as the negative probabilities were being shared, Caleb hushed the people and said, "Let's go at once to take the land ... we can certainly conquer it!" (Numbers 13:30 NLT). But the rest of the leaders ignored him and amplified the giants as the *giant* problem before them. Along with the illustration of the size of the giants, they had one more report to add. This report was about themselves. And they said, "We were like grasshoppers *in our own sight*, and so we were in their sight."

Need I say any more? This is not to deny that the giants and big walls posed a challenge before them. But the bigger problem was in their "own sight." They saw themselves as grasshoppers through their own eyes. Like many of us, including myself, these guys sure needed corrective lenses. They had convinced themselves that they were grasshoppers. They self-proclaimed themselves to have the likeness of an insect and also sold the grasshopper ideation to the giants, "And so we were in their sight."

Caleb, who called them out on their timidity, was certain that they could possess the land. The others were probably discussing their fears on the way back from scouting, and so Caleb wanted them to "go at once," before they got a chance to burst out their grasshopper story.

Do you tend to see yourself as a grasshopper? You need new vision. Have you tucked yourself inside your tent with depression, fear, and shame? Perhaps you need new relatives.

Much-Afraid struggled with her vision as well, of what she thought she was in her own sight? Her willingness and excitement to go to the high places with the Chief Shepherd was unmistakable. At the same time, she was consumed with her fear of her relatives. She was conscious and overcome with shame because of her appearance. She longed to be delivered from her physical shortcomings, which included a crippled foot and a crooked mouth. But she also couldn't bring herself to look away from her deformities.

She looked down at her malformed feet as she spoke, and her eyes filled again with tears and despair and self-pity. These mountains are so steep and dangerous. I have been told that only the hinds and the deer can move on them safely.   - Hannah Hurnard

The Chief Shepherd was ever willing to take her away from the Valley of Humiliation and take her to the wonderful heights of the High Places. She had His word. But her blemishes, her deformities, her fears—all had her chained to them. The Chief Shepherd - He got her there, as promised.

Are you willing to rest assured in the promises you received from God? Are you willing to believe that the promises in themselves, have the power to fulfill their assignment? All God's promises are complete only in Him. If we have His word, however difficult or impossible the promises may be, they will be fulfilled.

Come out of your tent, and on a clear, starry night, gaze at the stars above. They tell us about the magnitude of the promises that will be fulfilled in our lives. Look for the dim stars up there too. They are countless. Perhaps you may be able to help one of those dim stars to shine again.

And one more thing. Remember Caleb? After the grasshopper episode, he went ahead and took over that very same promised land at the age of eighty-five.

The promises of God do not have expiration dates on them. They can be claimed whenever we are ready. The voices of negativity and fear may have pushed him back. But Caleb returned and took hold of his promise after forty-five years!

CHAPTER 8
Hope's Task

The world breaks everyone and afterward
many are stronger at the broken places.
—Ernest Hemingway

All of the leading men and women we got acquainted with through the course of this book had all been broken—broken by their experiences, their circumstances, and people. Moses, Elijah, the woman with the bleeding hemorrhage, Hannah, Abram and Sara, Paul, and Corrie Ten Boom—they had all been in broken places in life. They were broken for themselves, and broken for others. And we watched God take their brokenness and use them as leaders, as deliverers, as answers to the cry of many.

They went from positions of power to weakness, from being overqualified, to not so qualified, from places of prosperity to places of want. And some of their stories start, from the broken places and hiding places. They had to all get to that place of brokenness for God to be able to use their stories as stories of triumph. They were all able to shine from their places of brokenness because that's where each of them knew that they had to depend wholly, only, on God.

For the duration of my struggle, as long as I was striving and trying to iron out issues on my own, I only added more frustration to my symptoms. There was a perplexity within me that I could not comprehend. The conflicting behavioral qualities about me brought me discontent and condemnation. And I desired to not act from that place—but I would end up doing it anyway. And the things I wanted to do, to get the right results—I would not do. This is perhaps how Paul felt when he was venting his frustration over his own clash between sinfulness and doing right.

> For I do not understand my own actions.
> For I do not do what I want, but I do the
> very thing I hate. (Romans 7:15 ESV)

Any understanding I had about myself, about who I am, tumbled and crashed. I felt like I was without an address or an identity. I knew that I could not rely on myself any longer to function from a place of sanity. Like I admitted earlier on, every effort on my part to make this sickening weight of depression go away, fell short. All of me had to start depending on God, for everything. From plain waking up in the morning to the ability to be mobile, to be able to eat and keep down what I ate, to sustaining sleep at night—nothing was left out. All of me had to depend, on all of Him. *Raw dependence* is what pastor Mark Batterson calls it: "Raw dependence is the raw material out of which God performs his greatest miracles."

Raw dependence will also require *raw obedience* - meaning we must be intentional about our dependence on and obedience to God. Because there is a strength that arises from our complete dependence on God during our time of weakness. That is why Paul acknowledged his weakness as a point of strength for himself—strength he could derive only from God.

> For when I am weak [in human strength], then I am strong [truly able, truly powerful, truly drawing from God's strength]. (2 Corinthians 12:10 AMP)

The book of Joshua is among my most treasured books in the Bible. The reason I can correlate with his story so much is not just because of his valor. It's more so because of who he was and because of his journey toward earning that title of valor. There is more to his story than just the tales of his valor. Joshua wasn't always courageous. The voice of courage and strength was generated in Joshua, from his obedience to God. It took reading the book of Joshua many times over to believe that Joshua struggled with fear. This is not a typo. I did intend *fear.*

Joshua was a silent follower of Moses's through most of Moses's life. Whenever and wherever Moses went to commune with God, Joshua was there, at a small distance away, subtly in the background. It wasn't until after Moses died that he was brought to the forefront as a leader. As I read the events of his appointment as leader and what was commissioned to him by Moses, by God, and by the people he was about to lead, I observed a pattern. I'm laying out each charge Joshua was given during his appointment as leader. You may observe the pattern as you read along the following verses:

- Moses appoints Joshua—Deuteronomy 31:7: "Be strong, courageous and firm."
- Moses instructs Joshua—Deuteronomy 31:8 : "Do not fear or be dismayed."
- God commissions Joshua—Deuteronomy 31:23: "Be strong, and courageous, and firm."
- God said to Joshua—Joshua 1:6: "Be strong, and courageous."
- God said to Joshua—Joshua 1:7: "Only be very strong, and very courageous."
- God said to Joshua—Joshua 1:9: "Have I not commanded you? Be strong and courageous. Do not be frightened, and do not be dismayed."

- People to Joshua—Joshua 1:17: "Just as we obeyed Moses in all things, we will obey you. Only be strong and courageous."

Is it just me, or do you see the flood of "do not fears," that Joshua received before he even commenced his leadership role? If you also notice, these scriptures were all in sequence as well, one after the other, and not that far in proximity from each other. Something tells me that he needed to be assured and reassured— that he didn't have any of those traits—courage, strength—at that time. If we read the Amplified Version of Deuteronomy 35:8, it reads:

> Let there be no *cowardice* or *flinching*, but *fear not*, neither become *broken* in spirit—*depressed*, *dismayed*, and *unnerved with alarm*.

As we keep reading further into the book, the scale of strength and courage rising in Joshua becomes evident. But at each front, he had to depend entirely and lean all of himself on God because such were the nature of the feats God had for him to accomplish. He had to have raw dependence. Every verse of encouragement to Joshua became mine as well. Fear was my biggest enemy, and if through raw dependence on God Joshua could progressively overcome his fear, then I had a chance at shaking this off too.

When depression took its toll on my life, fear was what was amplified the most. All the fears and relatives of fear that Joshua had—cowardice, flinching, depression, being dismayed, being unnerved with alarm—I had them all. Anything and everything I looked at, screamed fear.

Countless number of times, I asked God to take the fear way. And countless times, I felt confused and crushed when the fear wouldn't lift. As I started to study the life of Joshua, I found that every step of the way, Joshua nodded 'yes' to the unreal, outrageous feats God asked him to carry out. They were unreal, wouldn't you say?

Beginning with crossing the Jordan to the walls of Jericho. I can't help but think that Joshua would have possibly, secretly hoped to have Moses's rod, that was held up to split the Red Sea in two. Joshua may have even imagined being able to pull that off, had he had the rod. He knew how that worked. Hold up the rod, like Moses did, and the waters will part. But that's not what God wanted him to do. He asked Joshua to send the priests, in heavy robes, carrying a rather heavy box (the ark of the covenant) to lead the way into the waters of the Jordan.

Joshua ought to have had raw dependence on God to see that happen. Not to mention, the next task at Jericho, where they were supposed to bring the walls down, minus the use of any ammunition. He had to be in obedience first and then depend entirely on God to witness the feasibility of what he was asked to fulfill. And obey he did. At the command to carry through every unbelievable task, he obeyed. When God told Joshua to arise, he arose. When God told Joshua to go, he went. With every step of complete dependence and obedience, there was being built within Joshua a voice of courage, so much so that the one who was being repeatedly told to not fear, once, when engaged in a war with their enemies, ended up commanding the sun and moon to stand still. And stand still they did.

> So the sun stood still and the moon stayed in place until the nation of Israel had defeated its enemies ... The sun stayed in the middle of the sky, and it did not set as on a normal day. There has never been a day like this one before or since, when the Lord answered such a prayer... (Joshua 10:13–14 NLT)

Joshua and Elijah, both men with *weak natures like ours*, were able to suspend nature at their word. It brought me a great deal of relief to study the places of weakness and depression of these heroes of faith. These people I personified merely as heroic characters began to manifest as real people. Their struggles and their lives began to leap off the pages. They had all derived hope, from their raw dependence on God. Their strength, was derived from the same place. Joshua knew he was afraid, and he knew he had to depend on God. Had he not done so, we may not have had the name of Joshua to associate with the crumbling of the Jericho walls.

I learned from these lessons to transition myself from constantly asking God to take away the fear and depression, to depending on Him to overcome this giant. I began to lean into God with all my heart. I use the analogy of a ladder when I think of leaning on God. When you lean a ladder up against a sturdy wall, as long as the wall holds up, the ladder is perfectly leaned against the wall. It was not easy, this leaning. I had to purpose within myself and ask myself, "Am I going to stand there, crying and hoping the giant goes away? Or am I going to hit it smack in the middle of its forehead and bring it down?"

If it was fear that was threatening me, fear was going to have to be dealt with. I have never stopped feeling fear, to this day. I still feel fear. What I have stopped, is letting the fear bully me anymore. I don't let the feeling sink far enough, to where it gets me sick to my stomach. Now, when I'm afraid, I counter it with the word. When He asks me to step out and do what He wants me to, I'm still terrified—terrified of failing, of what people may say. I have just had to train myself to do it afraid.

God never said we wouldn't feel fear. He said, "Do not fear." With each step we take forward, afraid, the fear gets slowly pushed back, and courage starts to slowly seep in.

I can only wish that fear were the only culprit. For one of the other unfortunate gifts that depression granted me was despair. In addition to the fearful knot in the stomach, every day, I woke up to "When will this pass? How can I get away from this?" And when the dust from the muddle of questions settled, I would wonder if there was any hope for me. Dare I hope that this will pass?

A while back, we had a lamp base at our home that dropped and broke to pieces. It was just a lamp base, but it was sad to throw the pieces away. I couldn't think of a way to bind the pieces back together. Turns out, there is a way to put shattered pieces of pottery back together. It dates back to fifteenth-century Japan, where Shogun Ashikaga Yoshimitsu broke his favorite tea bowl. In his desire to be able to keep his cherished bowl, he sent it to craftsmen in China to have it repaired. But when it was returned, the repair was done by stapling the delicate broken pieces together with unaesthetic metal. Needless to say, it disappointed Ashikaga. He beckoned his craftsman to devise a more desirable solution to repair the bowl. The method they fashioned however, did not disguise the damage. Rather, it preserved the damage in an aesthetic way - using the art of Kintsugi, in which the broken pieces are joined back together, with gold. The result is a beautiful piece, that renders the broken lines to look like veins of gold running through this marvelously restored pottery, making the restored piece even more beautiful than the original.

This philosophy of restoring damaged pieces of ceramic, rather than throwing them away, or replacing them with something new, is simply fascinating. And it could gather some allegorical value to the brokenness some of us have had to endure. It renders hope to us that our brokenness is not something that has to be disposed. God "heals the brokenhearted and binds up their wounds" (Psalm 147:3 AMPC) and "saves the crushed in spirit" (Psalm 34:18 ESV). When God joins our broken pieces back together, the end product will add value and beauty. The lines that once showed brokenness will be the very cause for our new beauty and purpose.

Our bandages and scars carry evidence of what we survived. They are evidence to others who are struggling that they are not alone. Our bandaged and healed scars could give them hope that they are not going to stay injured forever. Our testimony could give them hope for healing. How would they know if we don't tell them? The scars from depression aren't transparent. We are going to have to make our scars transparent by sharing our raw struggles, together with truth-inspired hope. Hope was what I looked for throughout the time of my battle with depression, and so do other people who struggle with depression. They seek an outlet for hope. Some may even be afraid to hope, and they deserve a chance at hope.

The story of every single cancer survivor, is a story of reassurance and true hope to another person who's fighting cancer. The pink ribbons are celebrated symbols of support, strength, and sisterhood to each struggling individual and to those who thrived. That is what our scars are for. They are the pink ribbons and footprints of hope and comfort to one more person, who wakes up to one more morn of depression.

> The Father of sympathy, pity and mercy and the God who is the source of every comforter, consolation and encouragement, who, comforts, consoles and encourages us in every trouble, calamity and affliction. So that we may be able to comfort, console and encourage those who are in any kind of trouble or distress with the comfort, consolation and encouragement with which we ourselves are comforted, consoled and encouraged by God. (2 Corinthians 1:3 AMP)

When I say *footprints*, it takes me back to Joshua. God asked him to lead the people *through* the Jordan— not over, not around, but through. God wanted the priests, to lead the way, bearing the ark of the covenant over their shoulders. When they arrived at the brim of the waters of the Jordan, that was flooded at the time, as soon as their feet touched the waters, the waters rose, stood up in a heap, and backed away until the riverbed was dry. The priests who carried the ark walked over dry ground and stood with their feet firm in the ground in the middle of the Jordan. They stood there until all the nation had passed over to the other side.

If you read the text in the third chapter of Joshua, it says the waters rose up in a heap and stood afar. The water did not disappear. It was still within their sight, just heaped up on the side. I always wanted the depression in my life to go away—out of my sight and out of my mind. But these people had to go through.

Our problems may not always go away because, God wants us to go through them, for a season. He will know the purpose. Our problems may still be in front of us, but with God, we can go through them and on to the other side. Be that as it may, that the riverbed was dry, but when the people went through the Jordan, they were strengthened and prepared for what was waiting for them on the other side—the great wall of Jericho.

When we overcome something of that proportion, we grow stronger by what we overcame, and we're equipped for the next test. When we overcome the Jordan, we're equipped for Jericho. We may have a hard time being willing, but we will be equipped. We may be overwhelmed in the natural, but under the shadow of our God, we are coming at it from a vantage point of victory.

The priests here played a crucial part. They stood firm on the dry ground, in the middle of the Jordan, until all the people had passed over to the other side. Did you know that we are priests? The apostle Peter calls us "a chosen people. You are royal priests, a holy nation, God's very own possession" (1 Peter 2:9 NLT).

I call them word-bearers. They were carrying the ark of the covenant that housed the tablets of the ten commandments, which represents the word of God. And as word-bearers, if we stand firm on the word, stand firm in His promises, we will see the waters recede. Our problems may be heaped on the side, like a tower, but it cannot overtake us. I cannot vouch enough for the healing, delivering power of the word of God.

As I mentioned earlier in the book, when depression choked me to the point of not being able to articulate it, I wrote it down. The priests stood firm on that ground, with the ark still on their shoulders, until all the people made it to the other side. If we stand firm on the word, you and I, we could be the catalysts that cause many others to cross over from depression, to the other side—to freedom.

Depression could be anywhere around us. I mean anywhere, in the people around us. We may never know. It could be the person seated next to us at church, next to us on a flight, next to us at work, or even next to us at home. Our families, who are with us every day, struggle with grasping the fact that the person they love is struggling with depression. It's no fault of theirs. Even they are caught just as unawares as those of us who actually went through it.

I say this to underline the fact that most depression stories unfold behind stretched-out smiles and behind closed doors, as was mine. None of the episodes of depression that I divulged throughout the book were scripted. I wish I could say they ended in a few hours, days, or months. But no … these disturbing stories played out for over five long years. They ran on real time, and there were no breaks.

God uses our trials to gravitate us toward our purpose. Through each trial, we are refined and ready for greater, better works ahead. Nothing is wasted in the hands of our God—our trials, the scars from our trials, our imperfections, and even our mistakes. Moses's stammer was used to speak to the highest authority in Egypt, which was one of the most powerful civilizations in the world at the time. The result was the deliverance and exodus of an entire nation from slavery. Joshua's fear was used for leadership and to conquer some of the biggest obstacles that stood in the path of that nation. Hannah's barrenness was revived to give birth to one of the greatest prophets of all time. David's rejection from his family was redeemed to make him the greatest king in the history of the nation. And even his missteps and setbacks were used to pen the biggest book in the Bible – the Psalms, with songs of sadness and depression, as well as songs of hope.

During my battle with depression, it was David's songs of depression in the Psalms that rekindled my rapport with the word. If you're like me, you may have raked up your *whys*, for your struggle. And I did voice a considerable number of whys. Some of these below may hit home.

> How long will You forget me, O Lord? Forever? How long will You hide Your face from me? How long must I lay up cares within me and have sorrow in my heart day after day? (Psalm 13:1–2 AMPC)

> My God, my God, why have You forsaken me? Why are You so far from helping me, and from the words of my groaning? (Psalm 22:1 AMPC)

Jesus, cried out His why as He was suspended on the cross, bearing gashing stripes and scars. Sometimes heaven remains silent because heaven knows what is about to unfold after we have endured the pain for a season. His purpose for our lives, will be unveiled. Wouldn't it be refreshing to get to the other side, knowing that we have not left anything unfinished on this earth? That we have fulfilled every work for which we were sent here.

And our whys are all right by heaven too. As long as He knows that after our period of mourning, we still trust our hearts to Him. David would utter his whys, and then, after his Selah moments, he would rebound to affirming, "I will give thanks to the Lord," and "the Lord is my strength." We could receive the answer to our questions, and there is a possibility that we may not. Our whys may only be answered in the story of some others lives, that hears our story and finds hope … for their whys.

On one occasion, my friend Mia and I were discussing the *why* phase we both went through during our individual struggles. We talked about each other's meltdowns, which happened frequently during the depression spars. The both of us realized that while we were going through the meltdown phase, we avoided any sort of communion with God. We believed that we needed to spare God of our meltdowns. The days of crying and complaining would make Him unhappy, we thought. Only our faultless sides could be directed towards God.

Well, that's not how David and any of the others responded. If you are stuck in this swamp of condemnation, you need to know that God does not turn the other way on your 'why' days. He cares as much about our sulky days as He does about our good days. As my friend Mia now knows, she can spend her depressed days before God—"meltdowns with Jesus," as we call them.

Charles Haddon Spurgeon, one of the most prolific Baptist preachers in nineteenth-century England, author of over 140 books, had preached over six hundred sermons by the age of twenty-two. He was dubbed the prince of preachers. His sermons and teachings are highly sought after to this day.

Spurgeon encountered depression even while he was a young preacher. His fame was soaring all over England, and his congregation had grown so large that they had to rent the Music Hall in Surrey Gardens for their services. At one such service, there was a large overflow of people in attendance. As Spurgeon was ministering, someone cried out loud, "Fire." Panic erupted and sent people flooding for the exits. The commotion resulted in seven people being trampled to death, and several others were left injured. From here on, depression was his chaperon. In his book *Lectures to my Students,* he addresses the causeless, sometimes unexplainable nature of depression.

> "Causeless depression is not to be reasoned with, nor can David's harp charm it away by sweet discoursings. As well as fight with the mist as with this shapeless, undefinable, yet all beclouding hopelessness"
>
> - Charles Spurgeon

Even as he wasn't able to gather an explanation for his stinging melancholy, or find feasibility in fist boxing this invisible illness, Spurgeon still believed that the darker hours gave him strength to go on. He believed that his depression was being used as a medium of molding him for greater works.

> Depression has now become to me as a prophet in rough clothing, a John the Baptist heralding the nearer coming of my Lord's richer benison. So have far better men found it. The scouring of the vessel has fitted it for the Master's use.
> —Charles Spurgeon

These words of Spurgeon, David, and all the others we deliberated over, herald the truth that many of these esteemed ones, and many of us, have all been visited by seasons of depression. Granted, they may have been at different degrees for each one. What they remind us of is the actuality that they were not all always walking in wholeness. They too were dragged down by intervals of depression. And just like the intensity and stages of depression are different for everyone, so will be the factors that caused the depression.

Ill maternal health triggered mine. Others may have theirs triggered by more traumatic events. Some may develop symptoms, with no awareness of what may have provoked the depression. Some have explanations for the cause, while others are unexplainable. God used the lives of the people we view as exemplary, to reveal to us the vulnerabilities they had and the hindrances they overcame. They left us evidence that we can hold dear while we bear the brunt of our journey. They left us footprints in the sand. The words they transcribed in history gave us a view of their lives, inside-out.

There is abundant potential in your story and my story. We may see ourselves as flawed. But as we know now, God used people with their flaws. He sent them on assignments that He knew they would never be able to accomplish on their own. If you believe that you have been marred by depression or any other impeding event that has brought you to question your worth, place your marred self in the hands of God. Let God do the unthinkable, and the impossible, with your story. The pages in your story that you don't care to read, are the ones that will be used by God to write the next chapter. God has only begun to write your story.

"The Lord is revealed in the backside of the desert, while his servant keepeth the sheep and waits in solitary awe. The wilderness is the way to Canaan. The low valley leads to the towering mountain. Defeat prepares for victory."
- Charles Spurgeon

Spurgeon is illustrating here in trimmed words, the marrow essence of the journeys of spiritual heroes we pondered over in the previous chapters. David was the one who in the solitude of the backyard, kept his father's sheep. Joshua and Caleb were the ones who brought fulfillment to the wilderness journey by stepping into Canaan. Much-Afraid was the one taken from the low Valley of Depression to the towering mountain heights by her Chief Shepherd. David's desert, Joshua and Caleb's wilderness, and Much-Afraid's valley, were all markers of each one of their journeys, the stepping stones before their punctuated victory.

There is yet another marker in the story of Joshua that deserves reflection. The people had all crossed over the dry riverbed of the Jordan and on to the other side. While the priests were still standing in the middle of the riverbed, with their feet firm on the ground. God then asked Joshua to choose twelve men, one from each of the twelve tribes. Each had to pick a stone from the spot where the priests' feet were planted and carry the stone to the other side. God wanted them to carry these as a symbol of their miraculous passage through the mighty Jordan. As tokens to show their children when they asked for the story behind the twelve stones, at bedtime.

Joshua further decided to install a second landmark. He set up twelve stones at the spot on the riverbed where the priests' feet left imprints. The priests were stationed there until everything God had commanded Joshua to execute was complete. Those footprints were proof of the inconceivable that was accomplished that day. Even as the returning waters washed away the foot imprints that stood on the riverbed, those twelve stones preserved evidence of the extraordinary passage of a multitude onto freedom and onward to scale the next challenge.

When we have been through long journeys of depression and have been favored to transition to the other side, what can we leave behind as landmarks? Our stories—our journeys, our hiding places, our shame, our fears, our raw struggles, our raw dependence on God. These are all our milestones and our turning points. These milestones could potentially be turning points, for another's heartache. These are our footprints of hope for those seeking it, while they have yet to conquer the length of their depressive journeys—for those who are still on their quests for hope.

Hope is a continual process. We continue to hope and continue to expect. With each step we take forward in faith, we accumulate hope. And even as we accumulate this hope, we could be the channels that release our hope to flow to others. Just like the priests who stood their ground in the Jordan, to hold back the waters so all the people could cross over. They served as catalysts of hope.

Tikvah is the Hebrew word for "hope." Tikvah also means "expectation." Even as we hope in the Lord, we need to teach ourselves to expect—to wait expectantly, to hope expectantly.

> Trusting is being confident of what we hope for, convinced about things we do not see. (Hebrews 11:1 CJB)

Strong's concordance also defines *Tikvah* as meaning "cord." The root word for *Tikvah* is derived from the word *Qavah*, which means to bind together, to collect, to expect. It says it is the "straining of the mind in a certain direction with an expectant attitude." The word *Tikvah* first occurs in the book of Joshua, amid the story of Rahab of Jericho and the Israelite spies. The word *Tikvah* is used here in its literal meaning, "cord." It refers to the scarlet cord that was let down from her window as a sign, that Rahab and her family would be saved.

The scarlet cord was the covenant sign from Israel to rescue her and her kin in return for her granting refuge to the spies. The surveillance team was sent to Jericho to scan the land they were about to take over. One scarlet cord, became the hope of deliverance for a woman who would otherwise have perished at the conquest of her city. And she in turn, stood as the hope for her kindred.

Rahab herself may have had her fears of whether her hope would fail her, of whether the spies would keep their promise to her. Even with all her fears and doubts, she hoped, in faith. Our hope, could be the scarlet cord that rescues us and many others. When our hope is unmistakable, many others will be the drawn to the hope they see in us. Rahab's hope was in the red scarlet cord she let down from her window. And the hope of the people she had hid in her house, was her—Rahab. She was their conduit to freedom.

Our testimony could be the scarlet cord of hope for many. Rahab had not yet been rescued, but she still placed her hope in the liberating promise of the scarlet cord outside her window. She decided to share her hope with others. Hope will endure even in the middle of our struggle with depression. Grant it a voice. You will overcome, they will overcome, and we will overcome by the scarlet cord of the lamb and the word of our testimony of hope.

Laying in the hospital bed nesting my newborn, I did not have the slightest inkling that I would have to brace myself for several painful years ahead. And even if I had braced myself, I doubt I would have been prepared to face the blur and pain of the future role I had to take on.

The experiences and memories of the past may continue to pursue its sting. But this I know, both the experiences and memories of the painful past prepared me for the work God had for me. I may not have been able to brace myself for the interval of depression. But that interval equipped me for a future where God could transform my pain to a manuscript of hope. In God's hands depression was only the beginning.

Speaking of windows, if you remember the curtains that covered the windows in my home? I would keep them closed because the light from the outside disturbed me so. If you also recall the sign that my husband asked of God with regard to the beginning of my healing from depression. The sign he asked for was that, I would one day draw those curtains aside myself.

However, letting in light through the window, had to be preceded by letting light into the darkness of depression that had clouded my inmost self. The light of the Word, of persistence, of hope – had to infiltrate past the enemy barrier of depression. And when there was planted inside of me the hope to see past the dark clouds - that hope, said it is time to draw the drapes open and stream in light aplenty. Hope had to carry out its task, inside out.

Tikvah

תקוה

HOPE

Notes

Charles Spurgeon, *Lectures to My Students,* (Prisbrary Publishing, 2012), p.340, 341, 346

Corrie Ten Boom, *The Hiding Place* (Grand Rapids, MI: Chosen Books, 2006), p.64, 138

Hannah Hurnard, *Hinds Feet on High Places* (Tyndale Momentum, 1979), p.8

Lyle W.Dorsett, *The Essential C.S.Lewis* (New York, NY: Touchstone, 1988), p.322

Mark Batterson, *Draw the Circle – The 40 Day Prayer Challenge* (Grand Rapids, MI: Zondervan, 2012), p. 120

James Strong, *The New Strong's Expanded Exhaustive Concordance of the Bible* (Thomas Nelson, 2001), p.245, 301.

CPSIA information can be obtained
at www.ICGtesting.com
Printed in the USA
FFOW03n0950200218
45190470-45712FF

9 781512 781830